What Cancer Said

WHAT CANCER SAID

And what I said back

KELLIE NISSEN

Published by the Power Writers Publishing Group in 2023.

Copyright © 2023 Kellie Nissen

All Rights Reserved. No part of this book may be reproduced by any mechanical, photographic, or electronic processes, or in the form of a phonographic recording. Nor may be stored in a retrieval system, transmitted or otherwise be copied for public or private use other than for 'fair use' – as brief quotations embodied in articles and reviews, without prior written permission of the author.

ISBN: 978-0-6458010-2-6 (Print)
      978-0-6458010-3-3 (eBook)

A catalogue record for this book is available from the National Library of Australia

Cover design by Miriam Rudolph.
Front cover photograph by Mel Thornberry.
Author photograph by Gray Tham.
Internal layout by Andrew Davies.
Project Management by Jane Turner.

All emotional definitions sourced from APA Dictionary of Psychology
https://dictionary.apa.org

Disclaimer

Any opinions expressed in this work are exclusively those of the author and are not necessarily the views held or endorsed by others quoted throughout. All of the information, exercises and concepts contained within the publication are intended for general information only. The author does not take any responsibility for any choices that any individual or organization may make relating to this information in the business, personal, financial, familial or other areas of life. If any individual or organization does wish to implement the ideas discussed herein, it is recommended that they obtain their own independent advice specific to their circumstances.

Contents

What's with that tattoo on the cover?	7
Dedication	8
Why would I share my story?	15
Everyone has a cancer story	20
What Cancer said	23
What Cancer did	25
Denial	31
The way denial sounds	38
Shock	41
The way shock sounds	51
Interlude	53
The way people react	60
Anger	63
The way anger sounds	69
Determination	71
The way determination sounds	80
Hostility	83
The way hostility sounds	94
Guilt	97
The way guilt sounds	108
Anticipation	111
The way anticipation sounds	122
Fear	125
The way fear sounds	132
Gratitude	135
The way gratitude sounds	142
Paddling for Vi	144
And in the end …	147
Final musings from a dragon boat	150
Appreciation	152

It sits on my forearm, right where the chemo drugs were pumped into my body for four months – a statement of who I was and who I am, where I've been and where I'm going.

What's with that tattoo on the cover?

"I never thought of you as the sort of person who'd get a tattoo," a friend commented when I posted a picture of my brand new tattoo on my social media page.

"What sort of person would that be?" I asked.

"Oh, you know," she said. "But I never thought you'd get one."

Sometimes I quite enjoy being an enigma. I'd even go as far as to say that these days I deliberately go out of my way to do things that others may not expect from me. But only if it's something I want to do.

And I wanted that tattoo.

Not a piddly little one in a place where nobody can see it. Why would you even bother? Nope, I wanted it big. I wanted it front and centre. If I was going to sit for several hours while someone carved into my arm and filled it with ink that can't wash off, then I wanted it to be worth it.

And it was.

So worth it, in fact, that it graces the front cover of this book.

My tattoo and this book were not intended to be a joint project. One did not lead to the other. In choosing the elements of the design, however, perhaps serendipity was at play. For, you see, my tattoo embodies everything that my story stands for.

The pink breast cancer ribbon – unfurled and free.

The dragon – representing my sport and my team but also symbolising personal empowerment and change.

Purple – the rarity of the colour giving it an air of mystery.

And the violets – for Violet. My grandmother. My strength.

Dedication

My grandmother, Violet May Sullivan, was born on 6 October 1925, and grew up never really liking her name. She insisted people call her Vi, never Violet, and always introduced herself as such.

The word 'violet' carries with it a number of meanings and you can lean towards one or the other, but the symbolism I like is that of creativity, wisdom and sensitivity. As a plant, violets are apparently considered to be quite tough, but they are also a symbol of love.

Violet suited my grandmother perfectly.

To me, however, she was simply 'Nanna', or, when I was just learning to talk, 'Oong-ga'. We had this bond that is hard to describe, a closeness that was perhaps forged by way of me being the oldest grandchild but more likely by the fact that for the first couple of years of my life my parents lived in a caravan in my grandparents' backyard while I lived inside. They were saving for a house so both were working, leaving me with my grandparents for a good portion of my first couple of years.

Some of my earliest memories take place at my grandparents' house – a tiny, two-bedroom cottage on a large corner block in Braddon, one of the older suburbs in Canberra, where they lived for sixty-five years. Even after my parents bought their home in Dickson, I spent a lot of time at my grandparents' house – at least, that's what it felt like.

At times, evoked by a touch, a sound or a scent, I recall those little things that make you pause a moment and smile.

Sleepovers – scampering in to the spare room, toes and nose frosty because the heat from the wood stove didn't quite make it to the other end of the house. Snuggling under the flannelette sheets and scratchy blankets while Nanna sat on the side of my bed and read from *Dumbo* or *Snow White*.

Baked rice – the spicy-sweet smell of nutmeg filling the house and making my mouth water. Tripe and white sauce – with its weird texture I quite enjoyed until I found out exactly where tripe came from.

Haig Park – the crispy crunch of leaves and nose-tickly scent of pine needles as we walked together through the park to visit my great-grandmother. Her house always smelled funny, but her lemonade, poured into sparkly glasses, tasted of fizz, fun and family.

And I remember Nanna telling Pop off as he dabbed my legs and arms with a paste made of bicarb soda to stave off the itchiness from the mozzie bites every time he allowed me to linger outside too long at dusk. I loved how powdery my legs went once the paste had dried and how it had all rubbed off on the bedsheets by the time I got up the next morning.

What I don't remember is Nanna's breast cancer diagnosis, although I vaguely recall her being in hospital for a bit when I was fourteen. My mother confirmed that 1984 was the year Nanna had breast cancer the first time. She was fifty-eight.

There were many more cancer run-ins, hospital stays, operations and treatments over the years. Her second round of breast cancer – in the same 'breast', despite the fact it had mostly been removed the first time – came about six years after the first. Then, uterine cancer two years later, in October of 1992. It was the radiation for that last one that ended up causing all sorts of problems. Still, she soldiered on, with Pop by her side, my mum and my aunt – all of us there for her.

She hid a lot from us – her four grandchildren – when we were younger. Even later, when we were technically old enough to deal with life's obstacles, she'd say, "I don't want to worry you."

Then, much later, and maybe only to me, she started saying, "I've had enough. I'm not having any more operations." When she morphed from one to the other, I cannot say. It may only have been after cancer had strengthened our bond.

Of course, she did have more operations.

And she always pulled through them.

My mother told me once that Nanna was very sensitive and easily upset but for the most part I only ever saw the strong side of her – the caring, the generosity and the empathy.

Empathy. Not sympathy.

My understanding of the difference between the two is that to have true empathy, you must feel what the other person is feeling because you've experienced something similar yourself. It's a deeper understanding; much less superficial than pity. Empathy often comes with guilt that you can't do more to protect the other person from pain. If it's possible to have too much empathy, then that's what I'd say Nanna had.

When I received my breast cancer diagnosis, Nanna was living at Goodwin Homes, an aged-care facility less than fifteen minutes from my home. Up on the third floor, overlooking the front entrance of the complex, she'd been in a room on her own for a couple of years – a hard thing to take after sixty-seven years of marriage to my grandfather who'd been housed downstairs in 'The Memory Unit' before physically leaving her for good. Nanna had been through some major depression – and had battled a particularly distressing bout of the disease not long after Pop died.

And now, this.

"I'm not sure she'll cope," Mum said. "Should we tell her?"

Keeping it a secret simply wasn't possible. Nanna might have had macular degeneration and very limited vision, but she wasn't totally blind and would have noticed when I rocked up to visit sans hair.

Instead, we tried to pick the best time to tell her about my breast cancer diagnosis.

As if there's a best time to give someone news like that.

As with everything, Nanna took the news quietly. "Oh no," was her first response. "Why?" It was a question that didn't require an answer. Which was lucky, because not even the oncologist knew why.

"It's my fault you have this," she said on more than one occasion, when it was just the two of us.

"The oncologist said my cancer is not genetic," I'd explain again. "He said there aren't enough markers; that it's just a coincidence. An unfortunate one."

"If I could have the chemotherapy for you, I would."

"I know that," I'd say. "But I wouldn't let you."

"You couldn't stop me."

I knew she wanted to absorb everything for me, to make it all go away. When she'd had breast cancer, she hadn't had chemo; back then it was always straight to surgery and radiotherapy. Even for me in 2017, having chemo first was relatively new – and was only used for some types of breast cancer. The aggressive ones.

"I wouldn't wish chemo on my worst enemy," I said to her. "But, I'm tough. I can deal with it." Despite my reassurances, though, I suspect her self-imposed charge of culpability was a much worse aggressor to deal with than having poison pumped through your body on a regular basis.

We did discuss other things during my weekly visits. The usual stuff – the kids, my work, the nine-letter word, the crossword clues, the slop she'd been given for lunch that day and the ineffectiveness of the massage they insisted doing on her knee to 'fix' a severed nerve from long ago.

"You don't need to come every week," she said, once I was well into my chemo treatment. "Don't feel you have to come just to see me."

Like I wouldn't. I may have missed one week, perhaps. I didn't visit her because I 'had' to visit; it wasn't out of a sense of family loyalty that I went and sat with her every week. Being with her gave me strength but I also needed her to see that I was okay. And that I was going to continue being okay.

Why?

"Your children are not supposed to die before you," she'd said at my aunt's funeral many years earlier.

At my father's funeral, barely five years before my diagnosis, she reiterated her distress. "He was too young," she said. "Why take him when we're still here?"

I simply needed to assure her she wasn't going to have to outlive her eldest grandchild as well.

And she didn't. That much, I did right.

Throughout my treatment that year, I saw or spoke with Nanna at least once a week. We both had our ups and downs but that time was precious and nothing was allowed to interrupt it.

Interruptions happen though – and I never do things by halves, so this interruption was huge. It involved Italy. It involved dragon boating – the International Breast Cancer Paddlers Commission Dragon Boat Festival, to be precise. Over 4,000 breast cancer survivors paddling on the Arno River in Florence.

I was torn.

"You must go," Nanna said to me when I first mentioned it.

That was before she had 'a fall' and ended up in hospital with a broken leg.

"Of course you must still go," she said when she saw me hesitate and felt my concern about what might happen while we were away.

"Paddle for me," she said. "You can show me your medal when you return and tell me about Italy."

"Of course," I said, full of denial about what lay ahead.

We both were.

The day of our flight, I sat with her on the edge of her hospital bed. It was my birthday. We ate cake and talked.

"Don't cut your trip short if … you know …" she said to me a couple of times. "I don't want to ruin your holiday."

"And …" How could I say these words? "… don't feel you have to wait for us to get back."

We both knew.

I walked out of that hospital room, my heart heavy with the knowledge it would be the last time I'd see my Oong-ga. It's the hardest thing I've ever done.

We went to Italy.

Nanna went downhill.

The first day of the regatta I stood outside the gates, backpack over my shoulder, paddle blade resting on the top of my foot, waiting with my team for someone to let us in. Anticipation and excitement rippled through the crowd like the wake of a dragon boat.

My phone rang.

Everything stopped.

This was it. "Hello?"

"Would you like to talk to Nanna?" Mum said. "They're giving her the drugs today. It'll be the last time."

I moved away to the edge of the group. Turned my back. My hand shook and my knuckles whitened. Throat constricting, I waited while Mum passed the phone over, helping Nanna hold it to her ear.

"Hello, Kellie." Nanna's voice was withered and thin. She'd had enough of this world.

"I love you." It was all I could get out before I became incoherent. Salty blobs rolled down my cheeks as all the emotion I'd been holding in over the last year burst forth, finally free.

Over and over, I said it and listened to her echo it. People around me looked; some gathered, hands on my shoulder.

Later, as we lined up for our first race, one of the ladies called out, "We're doing this for Vi."

Nanna, we paddled for you. I paddled for you.

This book, with all my strength, is for you.

I love you and miss you more than you'll ever know.

Why would I share my story?

My name is Kellie … and this is the book I was never going to write.

For nearly five years, I had zero desire to share 'my cancer story' with the world. I was happy to talk about the year I'd had with people who asked but – let's be real about it – there are a lot of cancer stories out there. Mine would just be another one. And, in all honesty, it was twelve or so months of my life and I just wanted to move on.

In my business, I work as an author coach and have mentored a number of people who are writing memoirs. I know there are a range of reasons why an individual might want to write about their story: to raise awareness, promote their business, share insights, create connection, offer a different view, or sometimes just to offload and get something off their chest. A memoir might be something the author wants to share with the world or, at the other end of the spectrum, it might be something they only share with their closest family.

None of these reasons for writing a memoir resonated with me, so I pushed aside the suggestions and urgings of my friends and colleagues and went on living my life until one day, around the end of 2021, I realised I'd been subconsciously mulling over this memoir idea for some time and had reached the point where I couldn't stop thinking about it.

Damn.

What brought about this change? Was this just going to be my version of the 'Covid book'? Unlikely. The latter part of 2021 was when all the medical ups and downs started. I was getting little niggles – a twinge here, an ache there, blood where there shouldn't have been. My GP sent me for many, many tests, all proving negative for whatever it was they were testing. The line-up of medications, particularly the Arimidex, were starting to show their side effects. I was edging closer to that time everyone talks about – the pointy end of the five-year milestone since diagnosis.

"Why is that fifth year a milestone?" my doctor asked.

I shrugged. I had no idea, I just knew it was a goal people talked about attaining. The magic five.

As it turns out, it is a significant number if you're into statistics. It's also the point when you and your specialists start to go your separate ways.

In my case, it was my surgeon. "I don't need to see you again," he said.

It's like a breakup. These people have been part of your life for five years. They've seen you at your worst. Held your hand. Helped fix you. Then they dump you.

I walked out of my surgeon's room on the day we split up, incredibly emotional. It was odd. Getting there for each appointment was a hassle. Finding a park was a pain. His hands were always cold. Surely it was a happy moment, a sign that I'd gotten through it all. Yet there was a definite hole where that happiness should have sat.

Strange things happen in the final lead-up to the magic five.

Phantom stabs of pain.

Lumps that aren't.

The mutterings from an annoying internal voice: "Write that book."

Clearly, though, book aside, cancer was on my mind. Actually, cancer was more than just on my mind; cancer had developed an annoying and persistent voice in my head that would not shut up.

The thing that was cancer had become Cancer – with a capital C. A proper noun. An entity, with a voice.

A chat with my friend and fellow author coach, Jane Turner, confirmed what I'd known for some time. "If the idea won't go away," she said, "then it's telling you it has to be written."

Damn again. I knew she was right, if only because I'd given the very same advice to many of my own clients.

"I don't want to write a standard, run-of-the-mill cancer memoir," I said to Jane.

Of course I didn't. I'm not a standard, run-of-the-mill person. I appear to enjoy doing things the hard way and setting myself impossible challenges. What's more, I am the sprouter of a number of somewhat unpopular opinions and spent my year of 'cancer leave' sharing said opinions and thoughts on a blog I called *Write About Quotes*. I suspect nobody ever read these rantings. Still, I did get some enjoyment from poking the bear.

My paternal grandmother was a 'poke the bear' sort of person. I'd grown up knowing her as a tiny, sweet lady who was respectful and tolerant – until this bubble of familiarity was unexpectedly burst when I was in my early teens.

"Put a sock in it, pus-nuts," my grandmother said to my grandfather who'd been ranting at her about the lack of something or other on his plate.

My father and I were sitting at the dinner table and heard what she'd said, loud and clear. My grandfather, however, was none the wiser. He was deaf. His hearing aids didn't work so well, and although he could lip-read she'd foiled that by standing behind him to express her frustration and pass opinion on the state of his manhood.

Satisfied and triumphant after her impromptu outburst, my grandmother continued collecting the plates like nothing at all had been said. Me, on the other hand – my jaw had dropped in a truly clichéd manner.

My father's mouth twitched. "That's your grandmother," he said. "The real Edna."

"What was that?" my grandfather asked.

"Nothing."

On the way home, Dad told me she'd had a tough childhood and had to learn to stick up for herself. She may have looked harmless and gentile but nobody – nobody – walked all over Edna.

Later, she developed dementia. That's when her repressed self – the Edna that didn't let people walk over her; the Edna who said what she thought – came out. She wasn't violent and she never went out of her way to cause offence, she just voiced her opinion and didn't care who heard it.

From that first 'pus-nuts' moment to when she told a fellow aged-care resident to cheer up lest she sour the milk, I aspired to be like her: true to myself and what I believed.

Poking the bear.

Unpopular opinions.

You can't say that!

"What if," I said to Jane, "I gave cancer a voice? What if I wrote about what I really thought and how I really felt that year? Raw, honest, shock-factor stuff?"

"That could work," said Jane. "But who is your audience? What do you want them to gain from reading your story?"

I was getting a taste of what it felt like to be one of my clients. What was my story question?

"I want readers to get it," I said. Then the words just tumbled forth; all my pent up, withheld, unuttered frustrations from that year. "I want people who read my story to understand that it's okay to feel what you feel. That every emotion you go through is real and valid. That the only person you need to please is yourself. I want people who are going through cancer to know that it's okay to say no. Or yes. Or whatever they want. And for the people around them to know that they're appreciated but that sometimes it's not about them."

"I think," Jane said, "you need to write this book."

And that's how it came to pass.

The cancer story I was never going to write.

It all revolves around an epiphany.

Words I have uttered aloud.

Three simple statements, received and processed with looks of horror and pity and disdain and disbelief.

Yet, I stand by them for I know them to be true.

For me.

The year I had breast cancer was the best year of my life.

And the worst.

Ultimately, though, it was the year I needed to have.

Everyone has a cancer story

Think about it. It's true.

It might be your cancer. A family member's cancer. Your best friend's cancer. We've all experienced it or know someone who has.

The similarity, however, ends there.

Different treatment.

Different reaction.

Different end result.

One of the things I found myself resenting throughout 'my' cancer journey was when well-meaning people tried to share books, articles, videos and the like with me – about someone else's story.

"It may help you," they'd say.

But I didn't want to read someone else's story. Not then. Not at that moment. This was my story and would be unique to me. Yet, I smiled and nodded and muttered things like "Thanks," and "How thoughtful of you," and "I look forward to reading that; it looks very useful".

I'd learned about the 'nod and agree' strategy in my third year of teaching when a classroom teacher with no Japanese-teaching background was constantly trying to tell me how to teach a foreign language. The school librarian had taken me aside. "Whenever she's on her soapbox at me about how to manage the library," she said, "I just nod as if I agree with her and tell her I'll give it a go. Then I put her advice in the round file."

Best advice ever! You can move on. The giver of unsolicited advice thinks they've helped. The reluctant receiver of said advice can continue doing things their way.

Everyone's happy.

It works well in all areas of life.

That's not to say I don't enjoy other people's stories – I coach people to write their memoirs, after all. Tales from the lives and experiences of other people are usually fascinating, sometimes heart-wrenching, frequently surprising and often sobering, giving you room to ponder and reflect. A good story will spark a connection between the author and the reader, whether through multiple points of similarity or just one.

It was like being in the dragon boat as part of the Dragons Abreast Canberra team. Most of us are breast cancer 'survivors'. Some are 'supporters' who paddle alongside a survivor family member or friend. A full boat consists of twenty-two women: twenty paddlers, a sweep and a drummer.

That's twenty-two stories.

All similar. All different. All worthy of being told.

What if, I thought … what if I interviewed these women and incorporated parts of their stories into mine?

Turns out I was biting off a bit more than I'd bargained for. Not because it was difficult to get the stories but because it was near impossible to slice off the 'gold'. Every part of every story deserves to be told. And they will be told – in their own book, where they can shine. They deserve that much.

In the interim, I'd still like to introduce you to these incredible ladies throughout this book. A sneak peek, if you like. Their kaleidoscope of emotions stand both parallel and perpendicular to my own.

At the end of each chapter, you'll find snippets from their stories – tiny insights where they share how denial, shock, anger and all the other emotions played out for them as they continued living their lives with breast cancer at their side. Each and every one of those ladies did themselves proud as they opened up their hearts, shared their tears and laughter and, in the end, recognised that their story was unique and was worth being told.

I'm proud to be part of their team – both in the boat and in our shared story of cancer.

Every classroom, every workplace, every family has 'that person'. The person who is loud. The person who always needs to be heard. The person who dominates every conversation and makes everything about them.

For one year of my life, that 'person' – that voice – was Cancer.

What Cancer said

"What?" said Cancer, after I'd finally voiced my idea out loud.

"I'm thinking about writing a cancer book," I said. "You heard me. Don't pretend you didn't."

"Finally!" Cancer held up her gnarled hand to fist-bump me.

"Get back in your box," I replied. She needed to be contained. "IF I write this book, it's NOT going to be glorifying you."

"Of course it is," said Cancer. "It'll be the story of your year of hardship and horrible things. You'll try to tell your dear readers how you conquered me and came up smiling. But, at the end of the day, it'll be the story about the scars I left behind and how I'm always with you."

I pondered that last bit – the bit about the scars and how Cancer is always there, even after she's not. I hate it when others stomp on what I know to be right and end up proving me wrong.

But there was no way I was going to give Cancer the satisfaction. She was only partly right. She was right about the scars. She was right about the fact that she's always going to be there, hanging around and threatening to rear her terrible head again. But there was no way any of that was going to be the focus of my book.

"That's not my story," I said. "It's not my truth."

"Piffle," said Cancer. "What is YOUR story then? Do tell."

I'd only half worked it out. I knew I didn't want it to be just another chronological cancer story – from diagnosis to treatment and recovery. I didn't want it to be a tear-jerker or an air-puncher.

I did want it to make people think, to question, to argue.

I did want to acknowledge and give voice to the role of Cancer and her nine emotional minions.

"My story?" I looked Cancer squarely in the eye and savoured her slight quiver. "My story is how my year with you was the best year of my life."

What Cancer did

Every time you're on an aeroplane, you're obliged to listen to the recorded safety talk and watch the cabin crew go through the motions, one of which includes pointing out the little lights along the floor, on either side of the aisle. In the event of a disaster, the lights will apparently come on to guide passengers towards the exit and, hopefully, safety. We've all heard the spiel and can probably recite it verbatim, although, thankfully, few would have had the great misfortune to be required to put the instructions into practice.

Here's a thought worth pondering: how handy might those little lights be in other aspects of life? A set of lights to guide us through life to safety.

I tend to ponder on weird things when I'm thousands of kilometres in the air, trapped in a tin and hoping there won't be turbulence – not because I'm scared of dying but because the thought of potentially needing to spew in a paper bag in front of strangers and people I know is rather embarrassing.

Anyway, as I was driving past the airport early in 2017, a plane was just landing … or taking off. I can't remember and it's irrelevant anyway. What's important is that I was suddenly reminded of the lights.

Well, there you go, I thought. You have those lights in your life now.

Cognitive connections can be very odd. The idea that my breast cancer, which had only been newly diagnosed and was in line for the full attack treatment within a week, had been tasked with being one of those guiding lights was strangely comforting. Not in a spiritual sense, mind you; just in a purely metaphorical way.

I drove on. More aware of my surroundings and knowing I was somewhat lucky I hadn't rear-ended anyone in my absent pondering, I attempted to push those thoughts away and focus on the road and the peak-hour traffic. The thoughts soon returned.

Was there a reason for my cancer?

Not a physical, medical reason but more of a 'message from above' reason. Was I being told something? Worse – had I brought this upon myself? Was it my fault because of something I'd done, or not done?

Stop it!

I forced my mind to pack those thoughts away. Lock the door. Throw away the key, or at least bury it deep in my handbag where all 'lost' things reside.

Having cancer sucks. End of story.

It would hardly be helpful to speculate about any higher reason for this cancer having been thrust upon me, or the lessons it had been sent to teach me. I had enough to deal with in my professional life without adding in any deep, soul-searching reflection.

Bitterness.

Discontent.

Resignation.

I'd been ignoring all the signs for years – the ones telling me I needed a change in my professional life. And not just any change but a complete overhaul.

Denial, that's what it was.

I knew it – I'd known it for years – but refused to acknowledge it. In doing so, I defined it. Funny, that.

Five years before my diagnosis, I'd been given an extension at a school I thought I loved. I was thrilled. Soon after, for various reasons, I realised I didn't love the school – nor did I love what it was doing to my son. My 'love' was actually denial and fear of change in disguise, so I swallowed that fear and put in a request for the extension to be revoked.

"Well, that's a new one," the lady in head office said. "Nobody ever asks for that." She didn't go as far as to say "tut tut" but I could hear it in her tone.

"I'd like to apply for a transfer," I quickly reiterated before I recanted my request. In hindsight, it probably sounded quite aggressive.

"It's most unusual," she said. The 'tut tut' was more pronounced now. "Are you sure you want that on your record?"

On my record? That I'd changed my mind?

"I'm fine with that," I said.

"Hmm." Nails clicked on a keyboard. "And your reason for the request?"

How much space did she have on that form of hers? My reason could very well be the subject of an entire book.

"I changed my mind," I said. "Five years in one school has always been my maximum, professionally speaking."

More tapping. They were sniper shots. "Perhaps think more carefully before submitting a request next time," she snarked.

Tap tap tap.

Tap!

"Done," she said. "You won't be able to change this again if you change your mind."

"Don't worry," I said. "I won't."

The conversation I had with the principal was no less enjoyable, made all the more tense by the fact I was also pulling my two children out and transferring them as well.

But I did it and went into the new year with a positive outlook.

It lasted only a little while.

Having taught senior primary for five years at my previous school, I'd asked my new principal for a totally different grade level.

Two years later, I asked for another grade-level change.

A year later, I went part-time.

I took on different roles.

I became my own one-man band at school.

Nothing worked.

I loved being with the students once class started, but getting there was the hard part. It was a struggle that started first thing on Monday morning, even though I was working part-time and didn't officially have to go in until Thursday.

The system was fraught with cracks that frustrated me. It wasn't that I resisted change – or maybe I did because the change I saw happening did not marry with my pedagogical or personal beliefs.

Everything got under my skin. Teacher attitudes. Media. Politicians. Administration. It all irked me. So many issues. None of them, however, irritated me more than special needs education and the way the kids are treated. As a parent, I'd been advocating for my own children, particularly my son, for years and was finding the divide between 'parent mode' and 'teacher mode' increasingly smaller, to the point where I couldn't differentiate between the two.

And yet, I stayed in that system. Stuck. I never advocated for me.

Comfort breeds discontent.

I was firmly ensconced in my twenty-year-long comfort zone and it was becoming disquieting, affecting all other parts of my life.

And my health.

Being stuck is awful.

Knowing you're stuck and not doing anything – or not being *able* to do anything – about it is worse.

If I'm realistic and honest, it took cancer to get me to stand back for a year, take a look at my life and realise I wanted more. Cancer made me realise I was sick of being a 'yes-girl'. That I was sick of toeing the line and doing things I was simply not enjoying. And that I was sick of being scared of change and terrified of failure.

Without that year, I know I'd still be spinning my wheels on that stationary bike of life; still at school and still resenting the fact that I was there.

I also fully believe I'd have turned into the supervising teacher to whom I was allocated for my very first practical placement as a pre-service teacher. A supposed 'mentor' who walked into the staffroom where I was waiting to be collected, looked me up and down and said, "Get out now while you can. This job sucks. I'm getting out."

I swore I would leave if I ever developed that attitude.

I swore I would never let my dislike of the system get in the way of my core business: nurturing young minds.

And I swore I would never become that teacher.

Cancer made sure I didn't.

Like a worn childhood blanket or soft toy, denial was my safe space, always open to retreat into at times of uncertainty or paralysing fear.

Denial

***n.** a defense mechanism in which unpleasant thoughts, feelings, wishes, or events are ignored or excluded from conscious awareness.*

The lump was there when I had a shower after I'd been to the gym.

It was still there the next day as I washed the lake sludge off after a particularly splashy dragon boating session.

A spongey, foam-like mound, that lump sat in the lower part of my armpit, towards the back. It wasn't huge. Maybe the size of one of those tiny bouncy balls I didn't have the hand-eye coordination to catch or hit when I was a kid – or now, for that matter. Or maybe the size of a marble. I'd never been into marbles but suspect the lump was a similar size to one of the bigger ones. A tom thumb? Geez, I don't know. All I knew was that I felt that lump and that it wasn't there before.

And it wasn't going away.

It didn't hurt. I couldn't feel it when I put my arm down by my side. It was soft but had a definite shape. I could move it around a bit.

A few years back, I tore a calf muscle or ligament – something like that – just randomly while stepping out of the elevator on the ground floor of a Melbourne hotel.

Shit, it hurt! I heard the snap too – like someone had flicked me with a massive rubber band. "Fuck!" The expletive echoed loud and clear across the hotel foyer. It bounced off glass walls and caused the heads of fellow travellers and hotel staff to swivel in my general direction.

We were right at the start of our Western Australia road trip. Five weeks driving from Broome to Perth, then back to Adelaide on the Indian Pacific train. What the hell had I just done? Surely it could have waited?

I hobble-cried my way to check-in. Sat, in throbbing agony, on the plane for nearly five hours. Limped off the plane into Broome's stifling heat and finally, half a day after hearing the snap, got given a pack of frozen peas and a tea towel by the concerned receptionist at our accommodation.

"Oh dear," she said with a pained frown. "I can't believe we don't have any icepacks. I'm so sorry. But this should do the trick."

This lump of mine didn't hurt like that … but maybe I'd torn some sort of weird armpit muscle at the gym. Or, more likely, on the dragon boat. That sport is rife with all sorts of injuries, owing to the unnatural position you need to put your body in to paddle. I loved paddling despite the constant niggling aches in odd places.

Yes … that must have been it.

"Who are you kidding?" said a voice from inside my head.

"What?" I asked.

"A dragon boating injury?" If the voice had a face, the face would have been wearing a sneer. It would have been up close, with rancid breath escaping from unbrushed teeth and cracked lips. The face you step back from lest you wear its spittle.

"Probably," I said.

"Are you really that stupid?"

I knew that voice; I'd heard it many times before. As a child, it was in the playground, in the toilets, sitting on the floor in front of the teacher who didn't hear – or didn't want to hear – the whispers from behind me. As an adult, I refused to be intimidated anymore by the type of bully that roams schoolyards and feasts on the smaller and weaker.

"Piss off," I said, then shut the door of my logic right in its face – but not before I heard its grunted response.

"You can't hide forever," it taunted. "I'm going to get you."

It was the taunt of every bully I'd ever known. A taunt that used to scare the crap out of me when I was younger. The taunt that made me compliant against my will and disgustingly meek.

As far as I was concerned now, at the age of forty-six, those sorts of bullies never followed through. What does 'getting someone' mean, anyway?

I'd had the best start to my year.

The sort of start that tends to come around in irregular cycles – between 'hardly ever' and 'never'. Not quite 'blink and you'll miss it', but the sort of start that hovers and floats and darts in and out of consciousness, sprinkling liberal amounts of fairy dust and keeping the world warm around you.

We'd not long returned from our best 'coast week' ever – light and fun and full of smiles and laughter. As a family, we rode the waves together again and again, then sat in the sticky shade eating fish and chips, and realising, too late, the 'family pack' was no longer sufficient for the growing appetites of the teen and pre-teen.

The greasiness of the crunchy batter still lingered on the roof of my mouth. The adrenaline spike from yet another narrowly-avoided dump by a misjudged wave was still with me a week later. The week away refused to be dampened by the inevitable return to work.

Work. School.

I was my twenty-third year of teaching. Since the age of eight, being a teacher was all I'd ever wanted. I'd had a career of highs and lows; a constant learning curve. Often thankless. Often joyful and satisfying. I'd been part-time for two years – a personal choice that stemmed from my regular 'five-year itch' of disillusionment and the need for change. Only, this time that itch hadn't gone away. I'd scratched it so much it was infected.

There'd been rumblings of doubt in my mind for a few years about why I was still teaching. It was yet another voice, and only partially quelled by the move to part-time employment.

But this year … this year had the feeling of a comeback. A rediscovery of the passionate teacher who had been lost for a while. I was still part-time but had agreed to work double the days I had for the past two years. For the first time in ages, I was looking forward to getting back into it. There was an air of positivity.

Somehow, I knew this year would be amazing.

Nothing was going to make it otherwise.

Yet, there it was.

The lump.

Small.

Pliable.

Ominous.

Stop it, I thought as I dried off and got dressed after showering on that third day. It's a gym injury. Dragon boating effects.

Or maybe it was an odd fat-cell explosion. Don't laugh – it can happen. My husband has little pockets of them in random spots on his torso. His doctor said they were harmless.

"Hello?" the bully voice said. "Cancer? Just putting it out there."

"Don't be ridiculous," I replied. "Not cancer."

"Then what?" the voice mocked. "Hey, Denial, I have a live one for you!"

"Don't you dare judge me," I said.

"Go on, then. Prove it. Prove you're not in denial."

My hand hesitated over my doctor's number on the phone.

"I'm waiting."

"It's not cancer," I said as I pressed my doctor's number and listened to the ring. "You'll see."

"Indeed," the voice murmured as it closed the door of my mind behind itself with a firm click.

Deep inside, leaning against the closed door, Denial stirred. "Don't listen to her," she soothed in comforting tones. "She's just an attention seeker. You have nothing to worry about."

I sometimes wonder if I was born with a predisposition for denial. How much of my life had I spent in that state?

My father was a huge fan of music from well before his time, much to the ongoing chagrin of me and my sister. We were frequently subjected to the likes of 1920s singers such as Louis Armstrong, as well as crooners from the fifties like Buddy Holly and Fats Domino.

It was torture to have to listen to these records – yes, records – much the same as it's now torture for my own kids to listen to my music, despite it being what I consider a diverse mix of old and modern with a smattering of every style. Including (gasp) the aforementioned Louis Armstrong. Although, his classic 'What a Wonderful World' is one song I still can't listen to. It was played at Dad's funeral in 2012.

One of the songs I recall Dad playing frequently was 'The Great Pretender', released by The Platters in 1955. Dad would've been six at the time. I hadn't actually thought about that song in years, but it comes to me now as I wonder if I'm a great pretender in my world of denial.

Pretend you don't care about not being invited to a classmate's party.

Pretend you enjoy sitting by yourself on the cherry tree outside the teachers' staffroom at lunchtime, making up stories and singing songs to make the time go faster.

Pretend you're not deeply hurt when the principal you love and admire talks about how much he can't stand 'teacher's pets' while he seems to be looking straight at you, in spite of there being five hundred other little bodies in the hall. Ignore the flurry of name-calling directed your way for months after that statement. Fake a laugh when your teacher makes fun of you over it and the whole class erupts in malicious giggles.

Ignore the mean comment from a mean girl in Year 4: "Check out all her fat rolls." Ignore the cries and jeers from procrastinating tradies as you walk past worksites as a body-conscious teen. "Arroooo … what a dog." Pretend those hurtful remarks were not aimed at you.

After the birth of your second child, pretend everything is fine when nothing damn-well is and the words 'postnatal depression' whisper in the far reaches of your mind only to be suppressed by shame and the spectre of perfectionism.

Pretend your dad is not sick with an incurable disease.

Pretend you said everything you needed to say to him before he died.

Pretend.

"Pretend that lump is a muscle injury?" inquired the voice. "Or perhaps a fat roll?"

Pretend not to hear the voice as it refuses to be tamed.

Pretend not to know that the voice has a name.

And pretend that name is not Cancer.

Denial is an attempt at gaining control when you know you have none.

Fake it till you make it, right?

"Chin up," Dad would say when my pretences formed cracks that leaked out the fears and shame and self-loathing they held back. Just a drip, here and there. Never a flood. Control.

"You are beautiful," he'd say, "and clever. Don't you ever forget that."

I didn't forget his words. But I didn't heed them either, or take strength from them.

I had to wait several days for an appointment with my doctor. In that time, the lump niggled. I'd run my fingers over it in the shower. If it gets smaller, I'd tell myself, then I can cancel the appointment.

Some days, I imagined I couldn't find it.

But it was there.

"It's fine," said Denial. "I don't know why you're bothering. It's not that big. It's not sore … you're overreacting."

"But …" I said as my mind travelled to worst-case-scenario land. As I thought of my aunt, who'd smoked since she was fourteen but feared breast cancer for its genetic tendencies. She'd ended up with lung cancer, not breast. It travelled to her brain – never her breast.

It killed her.

A little part of you dies when someone you love passes. Nanna's words about the unfairness of your children dying before you echoed in my mind – what if your grandchildren die before you? Your eldest granddaughter?

And what about the impact on your kids? They're surprisingly resilient, but I didn't want that for my children. They were only thirteen and eleven. What would they do if …

On and on I went, creating new scenarios. New 'what-ifs'.

Imagination is a powerful beast. And somewhat spiteful.

I had to keep this appointment. Even if the lump disappeared as quickly as it had appeared, I had to see my doctor for my own peace of mind.

Because if it was cancer then leaving it unacknowledged would put it in control.

Knowing it was there and naming it would put the control in my court. At least in my mind.

I could deal with the rest later.

The way denial sounds

I didn't have a lump – it was more of a thickening.
So, I just decided there was nothing wrong and
went on with my life.

~ Clare ~

When I'd made the appointment for those extra tests, they
told me to make sure I scheduled the whole day to be there.
"We can't say how long it's going to take."

I couldn't believe it. As if it was going
to take the whole day – really!

~ Megan ~

Finally, we trundled along to the holding room outside the theatre. One of the nurses there asked me what I was having.

"A mastectomy," I said.

She shushed me. "You don't have to talk so loud," she said.

I didn't really understand. I hadn't spoken loudly but then I realised that she didn't want me to say that word out loud. As if I should be keeping it all a big secret; keep my privacy. I thought that was a weird attitude. Why should it be something to be embarrassed about?

~ Marion ~

The shock of it all raged through every part of my consciousness, switching off pain and emotion, leaving nothing but numbness and barely the ability to operate, let alone apply thought, logic or care.

Shock

n. a sudden disturbance of equilibrium.

"The radiologist is here today. He said he can do the biopsy for you now. Do you have time to stay?"

When is a question not really a question, I wondered. Of course I'd stay; I was already covered in sticky goop, boobs out, body balanced on the thin, hard table. The paper sheets under me were scrunched and the starched white towel draped over my top half felt cold and slimy. It wasn't a question at all. I really had no choice.

She passed me another towel. "To wipe yourself down," she said. "Stay here. Don't get dressed just yet. He'll be in shortly."

One towel is never enough. These ones had all absorbency starched out of them and were effective only to smoosh the goop around. Fully exposed like a slab of raw tripe on a plate, I held the towel in a gooey ball, unsure of what to do with it.

What had just happened?

Less than three hours before, I'd been laying in a similar – albeit less sticky – state of top-half nakedness in my doctor's room, staring at the ceiling as she pressed hard and deep over every section of my breasts. She'd found a lump. So deep, she'd said, she wasn't surprised I hadn't found it.

The breast lump's sibling cocooned under my armpit – not a muscular injury after all – was much less shy. Totally different in character, as many siblings are, it was more of an attention seeker.

My doctor made an appointment on my behalf, so I'd gone straight from the practice in Ainslie to Canberra Imaging with little time to spare for thinking or fear. Room for numbness only.

"Come through," the sonographer said, my bum having barely grazed the seat in the waiting area. Inside the stark room, I stood, half naked, pressed against the humming metal and plastic squeezy machine like a ham waiting to be sliced. My breasts were squished and squashed again, this time between cold, hard plates of radioactivity. They caused me to hold my breath and wait for what I was sure would be the inevitable 'pop', only to be released with a flop at the very last minute. This invigorating experience was then followed with the aforementioned goop-smearing and additional prodding with a remotely phallic-looking device. Google tells me it's a transducer – the handheld transmitter of an ultrasound machine.

Dignity is not a word that belongs in this scenario.

Three hours! It had passed so quickly yet felt like years of my life.

The radiologist – a grumpy-looking guy with grey hair and a thin nose – came into the room at some point and said some stuff my brain had no room to store, then discharged what could well have been a handgun for the noise it made. He exited the room with a mumble. His haste was matched by the warm river of what I assumed was blood flowing down the side of my body not numbed by anaesthetic.

"Let me clean that off," the nurse said as she scrubbed at the river with a damp towel. "The results will be with your doctor later today. Stay positive." She herself sounded anything but, and I was left in the room to disentangle myself from the wads of goopy, blood-stained towels and scrunched paper sheets, find my clothes and wrench them on over my damp body.

Somehow I managed to find my way out, down the maze of over-bright hallways, past doors labelled 'Do not enter' and out into the reception where they took a significant portion of my money.

The phone call came less than an hour later.

"Doctor would like to see you first thing Monday," said the receptionist. A note of sympathy tinkled at the edges of her otherwise brusque business voice.

It was Friday. For two days I'd be waiting to hear what I already knew, and had known since I'd first blamed that lump on dragon boating.

Two days to dream up worse-case scenarios and every possible conversation my doctor and I could have.

Two days to pretend not to worry or be scared or realise that everything was going to change.

Everything.

"Yes, but maybe …" said Denial.

"You've had your turn," said Shock. "Move over so I can think."

"But, you won't think," said Denial. "You'll just sit there all muted in your usual state of disbelief."

"Will not," retorted Shock, but her voice had already taken on a translucent tone.

"Move over, both of you." The bully voice, having been strangely quiet in its cocoon of smugness, now boasted an air of condescension. "Well, well, well."

"Well, what?" I said.

"Oh … you know." All sing-song smart-arse, through and through.

I slapped it away and found my deputy principal's number in my contacts. "I'll be a bit late on Monday," I said when she answered. "Not sure when I'll get in – should be by recess, though." It was fine. It wasn't like I had a class of kids expecting me. Only new kids and Kindies. Yet, not wanting to let others down was rooted deep in my psyche.

"Is everything okay?" she asked.

"Had to change a doctor's appointment," I half-lied. "It's all good – just a pain for everyone else. Sorry."

Long after we'd hung up I was still sitting at the kitchen table, phone in hand, staring intently at nothing. The silence in my head, the absence of voices, was disconcerting.

Monday morning came too soon. The weekend had passed – a growing snowball in which Fear, Anxiety, Anger, Self-Pity and Disbelief packed themselves tight behind Denial's firm boundary that kept my 'secret' from everyone around me. I was feigning normality.

I'd followed my usual routine. Saturday morning was spent at dragon boat training with my daughter, a few board games in the afternoon with my son and then time spent preparing for the school week ahead – maths for Year 5/6 and reading activities with my precious Year 2 ESL gang whom I'd nurtured and grown fond of since they were in Kindergarten. They'd shown amazing growth. A quirky, fun group, I loved my time with them. On Sunday I spent time with my grandmother, as I did every week; twice a week if I could.

I sat with her that Sunday, in her bleak room at the aged-care facility I hated. She missed my grandfather terribly. When they'd first come to the nursing home they'd been together in a couple's room. After some time, and when things got difficult, he was transferred downstairs to reside behind locked doors in 'The Memory Unit' – the facility's ridiculous name for what was really the dementia ward. It was the first time they'd been separated in over sixty years. She moved from the yellow wing, upstairs on the third floor, to a single room, still on the same level but diagonally opposite, in the purple wing. In some countries, purple denotes royalty. Not here. He'd passed away in his sleep not quite a year and a half ago. She told me she felt his presence often. At night, he'd sit on the edge of her bed, keeping watch over her. I did not disbelieve that; it was the kind of man he was.

We drank our beverages – coffee for me, tea for Nanna. We ate the muffins I'd made earlier that morning. We talked of my kids, of the upcoming year and of the shenanigans of the other residents in her corridor: the lady a few doors down who had scratched one of the carers that morning as they'd tried to dress her; the lady across the way who was told to "stay in your room and not come out"; and the gentleman in the room on the end who, it transpired, was one of the deputy principals when I was in high school.

Through our banter and the sussing out of the 'nine-letter word' in the day's newspaper, I knew she sensed something. I could see it in her eyes; hear it in her tone. But she didn't ask. She knew I wouldn't tell – not until I was ready.

Medically, my grandmother had been through more than her share of trauma. Multiple cancers. A hip replacement that ended in a severed femoral nerve and resulted in a lack of sensation in her left leg. By the time the surgeon admitted his error, it was too late to rejoin the nerve, resigning Nanna to a walking stick, then a walker. A shattered kneecap from a fall, never operated on because it was the left one and could not be felt. And now macular degeneration. It robbed her of the ability to do her crosswords, read magazines and watch her beloved horseracing and Saturday sport.

Still, she kept on.

As would I.

I left the facility later than normal that Sunday and did not sleep well that night.

So it was that Monday arrived, and still I followed the normal routine. On autopilot, I packed school lunches and bags, including my own. I kissed my husband before he cycled off to a job he was growing increasingly discontented with. I saw my daughter off on the bus to high school – her second year – and my son off on his short walk to school. He was in Year 6.

Nobody questioned why I was leaving later than normal.

I offered no explanation.

The house was silent and totally mine for the briefest ten minutes before I locked up and drove in the wrong direction – heading to the doctor instead of my school.

"Sit down," my doctor said. She didn't look directly at me. Couldn't, perhaps.

I'd known her for twenty years. She'd seen me through two pregnancies and all the childhood illnesses. Written countless referrals to paediatricians and other specialists. Saw me through a horrendous time with a physiotherapist who was milking the compo system after I'd dislocated my knee at school. Yet, she couldn't eyeball me now.

I knew. But I waited.

She fiddled with some papers on her desk. Smoothed her hair. Stared with intensity at some writing I couldn't quite see on her monitor.

Only then, when there was nothing else to do, did she look at me.

"Breast cancer." She nodded, her eyes soft at the edges. "It's moved to the lymph nodes – that would be the lump you found."

She waited then, a box of cheap, scratchy tissues in her hand. Waited while that flood came out of nowhere, punctuated with gasps and snorts, dripping salty wetness all over my shirt and then stopping with a shudder.

I knew.

I knew all along.

What I didn't know was if I'd be able to bounce back from this.

No certainty. No timeline. No guarantees.

No control.

That last thing, the notion of it being 'out of my hands', was what really scared me.

That's why I cried.

It's what I told myself, anyway.

With my face prickling in tight, red blotchiness, I listened as my doctor explained what I had to do. I watched her write me a referral. I waited as she rang to make me an appointment with the surgeon.

"He can fit you in at 4 o'clock today," she said, her hand over the mouthpiece. "Can you get there then?"

Another choice?

I nodded.

She wrote the name of the surgeon's rooms. His name. His number. "He's the best," she said. "You'll be in good hands."

I have no recollection of how I got home. One minute I was at the reception desk, the next I was in my kitchen.

I contacted my husband. Spoke briefly. Just the facts.

Rang my school, even more briefly.

Allowed the answering machine to deal with calls.

Sent monosyllabic responses to text messages.

I sat.

Stared into the blankness behind my eye sockets.

Probed at the offending lump.

Gazed at the wall.

At 3:15 pm, I got into the car and drove to the surgeon's rooms.

"Is it just you?" he asked.

His office was massive. Desk up one end, examination table down the other. A big pull-around curtain. Enough room for a family gathering.

"Just me," I said. My husband had been tasked with being there when the kids got home. Also tasked with telling them, because I knew I couldn't.

The surgeon nodded. "Chemo first," he said. There was no beating around the bush. I liked that. "Then surgery. Then radiotherapy." He wrote down a man's name – a double-barrelled surname. "This oncologist – he's Canberra's best. If he agrees with my suggestions, we'll proceed. Do you have any questions?"

No questions.

He stood and walked me across his room. Opened the door.

"Ring if you need anything," he said.

More tears as I sat in the car.

Three times, I started the engine then stopped it. Too dangerous to drive when you can't see.

Eventually, dry-eyed, I somehow managed to navigate the peak traffic in the half-hour drive home without taking a wrong turn or rear-ending the car in front of me.

Autopilot.

My companion – the voice I now knew the name of – maintained her relentless chatter, a cross between the righteous crowing of a playground bully as she chalks up another win and a small blunt chisel chipping away at my hope and resolve. I lacked the strength of mind to silence her.

Denial was no help as she'd skulked away to a dark corner to lick her wounds.

Shock had wrapped herself around me until I'd been mummified in thick cotton wool, everything around me drowned out and distant – except that voice. Cancer.

I allowed Cancer to continue her monologue, white noise in the background.

By 5:15 pm I was home.

A silent house.

Solemn-faced kids.

Husband's hand on my shoulder.

Hugs returned with feigned enthusiasm, my arms like planks of wood.

Shock took one last stand – but she was weak, her strength spent and washed away in tears.

This could not be happening.

But it was.

It had taken nine hours for the rest of my year to unfold and spread out like a map in front of me. A new map with no key. My previous map – the one I'd had a mere nine hours earlier, that was carefully orchestrated and much anticipated – crumpled, then shredded itself. It had no further use.

Nine hours.

And now Cancer stood before me. She shook her ugly head and scowled. "I'm in control now!"

It hit me then.

Everything was out of my control. I'd spent the day – the last week – being pushed and pulled from pillar to post. Poked and prodded and probed. I'd been talked at and about, but not really 'to'. Already, I was a number. A percentage. A size. A probability. For now, I had no say because I had nothing to contribute. This was not my field of expertise.

Thus, everything was out of my control. Strangely, though, that much I could deal with. It's what the medical profession is for and why we put our trust and faith in them.

Still, I was crushed.

Deflated.

Despondent.

Why?

It wasn't so much what Cancer said, but the attitude with which she'd said it.

Shock walks many paths. A multi-talented emotion, it seems to be the ultimate protector.

In the event of good fortune, shock acts as a seatbelt, keeping us strapped in tight lest we go overboard and hurtle through the windscreen, crossing the line between joyful anticipation and over-reaction, or modesty and arrogance. In doing so, shock then moves us, without warning, from the heights of elation to the depths of despair.

I'd worn the seatbelt many times.

My initial offer of permanency from the Department of Education in a year where an extraordinary number of my peers were only offered short-term contracts. No way! It must be a mistake. It's only because …

Opening that email to see the words: *We're pleased to let you know you are the sole recipient of the 2019 Anne Edgeworth Fellowship.*

What?

They must have sent this to the wrong person. Are you sure? I was so underprepared and waffly; no way was it me.

So too had I worn the bandaid of shock which covered my wounds until they started to scab over, ensuring infection did not set in before the body could begin its healing.

My grandfather's gradual decline in the claws of Alzheimer's.

Dad – the most wonderful, caring and generous of men – passing before his time thanks to the tiniest of fibres that had chosen his lungs as their resting place, gradually reducing his ability to breathe and robbing him of the joy of seeing his grandchildren grow.

And now, Shock was reinventing herself as the pause button on the game of life. A temporary measure to allow me time to process what had just occurred and what was yet to come.

Twenty-four hours later, I responded to Cancer's crowing about her position of control.

I stood tall in my mind.

I took a deep breath and from deep in my diaphragm I allowed Anger to join the party. Together, we summoned two words.

"Fuck you!"

The way shock sounds

It was very confusing. My husband said later that he realised what was being said, but the message didn't sink in at all with me.

~ Anita ~

That day, three people cried when they saw me. I was in the middle of chemo and had no hair and I suspect it must have been quite a shock, but still, you don't want people to cry when they see you. I just wanted to say, "I'm getting on with it, guys. It's fine."

~ Deb ~

And so, a short period of nothingness descended; a period where one merely went through the motions, as if on autopilot, and the immediate world shifted slightly in adjustment.

Interlude

***n.** an intermediate performance or entertainment,
as between the acts of a play; a period of inactivity; lull.*

There wasn't much I was certain about during the early days except that I didn't want to be a burden on anyone, least of all my colleagues. Why school would be the first thing I thought of, I do not know. What I did know was that I needed to take leave. And that leave needed to be for as long as it took for this whole sorry story to be over and done with.

"Scared you won't cope?" asked Cancer. "Worried about being at work with no hair?"

I thought about it and was annoyed to admit that Cancer was partly right. I'm not a vain person usually, but I was buggered if I was going to face up to school every day with no hair. Or worse – a wig that clearly wasn't my own hair.

"Everything was fine except the hair loss," one of my teammates, a breast cancer survivor herself, told me. "Your hair is your identity. It's your strength. When it's not there, people treat you differently and you see yourself as something less."

So, yes, the hair played a part in my decision. A small part. There were bigger things at play. The old chestnut of not wanting to let people down. Relief teachers were hard to come by at the best of times, even with weeks of advance notice, let alone first thing in the morning of the day you're supposed to be working.

No. It had to be all or nothing.

I wouldn't be any use to anyone if I kept plodding into work every day, just doing the best I could. Students need consistency, not the uncertainty of 'maybe our teacher will be there and maybe she won't'. It was better for the school, and for me, if I just called it at the start and took extended leave.

I said this to myself.

I said it to Cancer.

And then I said it to my principal.

Cancer huffed in a self-satisfied way; my principal nodded with sympathy and a modicum of relief. I felt a curious mix of freedom and guilt.

Moreso than many who find themselves in my situation, I was incredibly lucky. I knew this. Paid personal leave was something I had in abundance, accumulated over close to twenty years of rarely being sick and having a husband who was able to work from home should the kids be too unwell to attend school. I had enough to see me through the whole year and there was no better time than the present to use it.

Once the word got out that I had breast cancer, my world became flooded with good-intentioned-yet-patronising platitudes, sympathetic glances and well-meaning advice from friends, colleagues, associates and the occasional family member.

Not all responses were unwelcome. As with everything in life, the way in which people reacted came at me in a mixed bag, not unlike a lucky dip at a school fete.

Some made me smile.

"Come over," said one friend. "Come and rant and scream and cry and stomp your feet until you get it all out of your system. Then come again and rant some more."

"Here," said another friend, passing me an exquisite notebook of her own design. It had blank pages. Was unlined. "Doodle, scribble and write," she said. "It's a swear book. It will listen and not judge."

I did neither, but the offers and intent and understanding of me melted some of the resentment and self-pity I felt, allowing me to move forward.

These two friends knew me. They acknowledged the need for outbursts and frustration to deal with the pain and the shock.

Then there was the sound of silence. This was like a punch in the chest. Those who I knew 'knew' but from whom I didn't hear a word. Not a text. Not a call. Not a card. I tried not to let it concern me. Everyone has busy lives. Everyone has different ways of dealing with things.

"She doesn't know what to say," said one friend about a silent one. "She feels uncomfortable. She's scared she'll say the wrong thing."

I tried to understand, but inside I screamed, "Who the fuck is this about anyway? I'm the one with the cancer and *you're* scared and uncomfortable?"

It was upsetting. It hurt me more deeply than I was ever willing to admit.

Is saying the wrong thing better than saying … nothing … at … all?

My eyes were opened to the disconcertingly large group of people who suffer from the 'I know someone who' affliction. They belong to the same group as the breastfeeding bandits, the 'my-kids-did' group and the 'I've-been-to-school-therefore-I-know-how-to-teach' crew. These people feel they are helping by sharing stories that are not their own but the stories of someone else they may or may not know.

You've met these people. Their conversations start with: "You should …" or "My brother's wife's friend had …" or even "Surely you're not doing …"

On the exceptionally rare occasion, the advice is good. Like the advice from my husband's colleague's friend's wife who'd had breast cancer herself the previous year. "Fruit Tingles," my husband relayed. "Apparently Fruit Tingles get rid of that ever-present metallic taste brought on by the chemo drugs."

She was spot on, actually, and I thank her for it – as should the suppliers and distributors of Fruit Tingles. Perhaps I should take out shares in the company because I give this advice to everyone who asks.

However, in most instances the advice that came my way thick and fast was, for the most part, useless, irrelevant and certainly unsolicited. It often punctuated those awkward gaps in conversation between two people who are yet to realise they don't really know each other.

Occasionally, said advice came via the human equivalent of a carrier pigeon – a family member or friend tasked with the transmission of words from another who either didn't know me or had not the inclination or guts to deliver the comment to my face.

Worst of all were the comments and suggestions posted directly onto my Facebook timeline by 'friends'. These were not the funny memes and cartoons that often made my day but the Facebook (mis)information on miracle treatments or the causes of the dreaded C. Let's just say that the power of muting or unfriending is a glorious thing and cannot be underestimated.

Offers of help came forth in waves. Some of them I took. Others I refused.

The refusals, and the variety of responses to these, told me more about the people who'd made the offer than I could have learned in a lifetime of conversation. Many people simply nodded and reminded me they were a phone call away should I change my mind. Others were offended. I kid you not. I felt their thoughts: "How dare you refuse my kind offer of help in your time of need, you ungrateful sow!" and "This is about you helping me feel good. Thanks for not caring about my needs." Nobody actually said that to my face, obviously; however, the stare, the tightening of the jaw, the abrupt harrumph and often the further lack of correspondence spoke volumes.

Some persisted despite my initial refusal.

"Just let us do this," two friends, colleagues from my school, appealed, "we want to. The staff want to help."

I'm quite sure that for some of my colleagues there was a sense of obligation but, obligation or not, the insistence of my friends that they create a meal roster ended up being a godsend for which I am eternally grateful. This roster, with homecooked meals delivered every few days, took so much pressure off me and my husband. We'd both felt embarrassed about accepting it. We both felt we could 'cope'. However, it wasn't long before we realised how beneficial it was. Although, in all honesty, I can say we have never eaten so much lasagne in the combined span of our lives as we consumed in that six-month period. My son referred to my friend who did all the deliveries as the 'lasagne lady' and it was a good couple of years before I felt like eating lasagne again.

I refer to this period of time as an interlude.

It's the dead zone between diagnosis and the start of treatment.

A period of time where your life becomes little more than a schedule of appointments for scans, blood tests, more scans and information sessions on chemo, breast care, radiation – an information overload.

Within three weeks, I had accumulated enough paperwork from various sources to potentially carpet my floor – or maybe wallpaper the walls of my study.

At the end of the three-week hiatus, everyone who 'needed' to know what was going on knew. Some people, I'd told directly – my immediate family, close friends. A few found out through family or colleagues; a couple through 'the grapevine'. However, I feel the majority of people – associates, distant friends and so on – found out through my Facebook post a few days after I was officially diagnosed.

Facebook! Yes. Social media – the great communicator. Convenient. Free. And you can cry a bit when you're writing a post and nobody is any the wiser.

> To stop people wondering ... (and I apologise to those of you who are finding out this way) ... I was diagnosed with breast cancer on Thursday (and it has spread into the lymph node) ... it has been the shittiest week but I have survived it (and will continue to do so) with the love and support of my colleagues at Aranda, my team mates from Diamond Phoenix, my family and all my other friends from different parts of my life. So many people have been so wonderful already and I thank you all. (You know who you are, I hope.)

I had a table full of flowers. Beautiful big bunches sent by my colleagues, my dragon boating club and an assortment of friends and family from interstate and overseas. They arrived day after day in a mini flood and then stopped, as if knowing we'd run out of room to place them.

My dragon boating team, Diamond Phoenix, were particularly wonderful.

From the day I 'publicly announced' my breast cancer, they were there. Several team members came forward – they'd had breast cancer themselves and I hadn't known. Why would I? It's not like you get a tattoo on your forehead of a pink ribbon and the words 'cancer survivor'. These ladies surrounded me and my daughter and also gave us space. They didn't drown us in advice but gave us a safe place to belong.

The timing of this stupid diagnosis had been just right. Yep – I just said that. If it had come a couple of weeks later, I mightn't have been able to attend the most wonderful Dragon Boating Festival at Darling Harbour in Sydney. It was before any medication or treatment had started so I still felt like myself, save for that lump in my armpit and … Cancer.

"Enjoy your last hurrah," Cancer mocked. "I'll be here when you get off the boat."

"I'm sure you will," I said.

My team had rallied around me and my daughter, cocooning us in a protective bubble of support and laughter. We weren't a Breast Cancer Survivor (BCS) team, but several of the ladies had 'been there, done that' and they and their daughters took us both under their wings and said words we both needed to hear. Words that varied from the specific to the general – all part of a normal regatta but slightly cancer-themed.

"Just be you and do what's right for you."

"Don't let it define you."

"What do you want to know?"

"Cancer sucks!"

"Shit, it's hot!"

And it was hot. It topped forty-two degrees that day, with very little shade and no breeze in the concrete jungle of Darling Harbour. Possibly, I should have worn a hat.

"But, I hate hats," I said when someone on the team mentioned that. "They give you flat hair."

I wouldn't have to worry about that in a few weeks.

Teaching and school seemed a distant memory. I speculated that this is what retirement must be like – being on holiday, without the spectre of class preparation or marking to dampen your enjoyment and relaxation.

It was something I could get used to. Without the interruption of medical appointments, that is.

The interlude was a necessary evil. On the one hand, it gave me time to adjust and to get things sorted out. On the other, it gave me time to think. To wonder. To fear.

At the latter times, Cancer would stir. She'd smirk. She'd open her mouth to speak but I'd turn away and distract myself with some trivial thing, leaving her to smoulder in her own negativity.

My husband was stoic. As was my mother. It was their role – the supporters. Someone needs to be the strong one. At the time, I was very full of my own self, my needs and my emotions. The little emotional space I had left went to my kids, both of them of the age where they walked the line of understanding and not. I worried about them; I feared the long-term effects of seeing their mother like this. But the greatest fear – the fear of 'What will happen to them if I cease to be?' – was the fear I refused to face.

As for other family members and close friends, I had no space for their emotions and just had to hope that the people I cared most about would be able to pull through.

Nanna was the exception. I spent a lot of time visiting her. An aged-care facility that smells of urine and decay is not the most uplifting of places to spend one's time but I would do anything for my grandmother. And I needed to be with her.

We were connected.

And now, we had another connection. Something else we shared.

The way people react

What I have subsequently learned, however, is that there are two types of people. There are the people who are supportive – they're the ones you want in your inner circle. Then, there are the people who you have to help in order for them to get through what you're going through. These are the people you want in your outer circle.

~ Kathy ~

Some people just know, instinctively, what to do and
say. Just before I started chemo, one of my best friends
took me over to the place in Holt where you can
buy wigs and hats. I tried on all sorts of headwear –
and so did she. It was a serious thing but somehow she
made it fun. I don't know how she knew I needed that.
I didn't even know I needed that.

~ Amanda ~

Brewing in a bubbling cauldron teeming with unspoken hurt, the dread of not knowing and the tedium of coping, my anger threatened to explode and shower all around with its pain.

Anger

***n.** an emotion characterised by tension arising from frustration or perceived injustice.*

Frustrated, annoyed, peeved, pissed off, impatient – however you wish to say it, I find myself experiencing some level of that emotion we call anger with more frequency than I know I should.

Anger hitched a ride along with the reactions and responses I had from those around me during that period of interlude. Like the parasite it was, Anger fed off every emotion, every comment and every reaction that hurtled my way.

She grew when people spoke but did not listen, or listened but did not hear.

She feasted on the do-gooders who 'knew what I was going through'.

She gorged on those whose help I needed, making me feel needy and reliant.

Above all, Anger had a field day with my grandmother's conviction that my pain and suffering was somehow her fault.

I tried not to allow Anger to lay herself out in front of these people. Instead, I attempted to placate her with words like "They mean well" and "They don't know that fifty other people have asked me that same question" and "You would do the same for them".

It was a struggle to keep Anger hidden. She was extremely well fed but it was never enough. Her appetite knew no bounds, and like some dogs she found it hard to stop when she was full. Thankfully, though, she did slumber at times. Even hibernated for short periods where she seemed satisfied with the slow feed of my personal running commentary of frustration, disgust, contempt and grief as I progressed through my treatment. Frustration at not being able to train at the gym the way I wanted. Disgust at the way I looked. Contempt for everything I saw in myself, from the way I spoke to the decisions I made. And grief … a deep sadness at what I'd temporarily lost and what I potentially stood to lose in the future.

For the most part, Anger maintained an ongoing monologue that was sometimes the star of the show but more often the background music. She sang 'the song that never ends', fuelled my stream of consciousness so it never ran dry and ensured the tap with the unfixable leak dripped, steady and rhythmic, drilling a hole into my brain and slowly …

sending …

me …

mad.

I've always admired people who manage to stay calm, using a measured tone and considered words in times of high stress. Yet, at the same time, I want to shout at them, "Tell me how you *actually* feel!" I want to stomp my foot and demand, "Stop giving me the unemotional, reasoned response!"

I'm aware of what I'm really saying: stop making me feel bad about my response to this situation; stop showing everyone that I'm the immature, overreactive one who's blown everything totally out of proportion.

Awareness, however, does not necessarily lead to control.

A little anger is a good thing, apparently. I suppose it is. Anger can motivate people to find solutions to problems. It's a protective emotion – a natural and automatic response to pain, whether it be from rejection, loss or fear. Maybe that was why I was angry? To protect myself. To motivate myself to get through that year.

I could spend the rest of my days analysing myself in this way.

Why am I so prone to outbursts and fits of pique?

Or, even more perilous for those around me, why do I resort to the 'quiet voice' when I'm truly off the charts? This quiet tone is the heavy hand holding down the lid on the overfilled pot of boiling stew, lest said stew bubble and spit and explode sky high, showering all around.

I could spend quite some time writing about pain instead. Emotional pain and how it feeds anger.

The pain of never feeling like I belonged. The pain associated with the awareness that I was somehow a bit different from my peers. The pain of being shy to the point of rudeness. The pain of not loving myself for who I am. The pain of not believing my father's words when he told me he was proud of me and that I was clever and kind and caring and strong.

Anger is much easier to feel, particularly when your whole world seems to have suddenly crashed down around you, the detritus laying at your feet in an irreparable state.

Anger knows this – and takes advantage of the situation.

"It's not genetic," my oncologist said.

Me and my ticking time bomb had only had to wait a week or so – another weekend – to get in to see him. In this time, all aforementioned comments had been delivered umpteen times but had yet to hit their stride.

"You don't have enough genetic markers for that. It's pure coincidence that you have it and your grandmother had it."

"Then how?" My husband, normally silent, asked this question. The one I couldn't, or didn't want to ask.

"We can't be sure. It could have been the pill." The oncologist's blue eyes pierced directly into mine. His voice, craggy face and flyaway hair reminded me of Sir David Attenborough. "How long did you say you were on it? Without a break?"

And there it was. Evidence. I'd done this to myself.

There were several other reasons he listed but I remembered none of them. I only heard one.

"It's your fault," said Cancer, only reiterating what I already knew. "You did this. You have nobody to blame but yourself."

I did not argue. I needed someone or something to blame for this gross disruption to my life. It might as well be me.

So, I let the rage simmer and bubble and build.

It was the boiling stew again. At times, the greasy gravy of my anger would rise to the very rim of the saucepan. I'd catch it, give it a stir and lower the temperature. Inevitably I'd lower it too much so it barely bubbled, and then I would swear at the injustice of it all and wrench the dial up high. As my back was turned, it boiled over before I could catch it, overflowing and pouring across everything within reach – my family, my friends, my acquaintances.

All well-intentioned.

All caring.

All unsuspecting.

All equally as unsure as I was how to navigate this new pathway. The blind leading the blind.

"You do realise that anger grows your stress and stress grows your cancer?" said Cancer, who had clearly been reading the bullshittery someone had kindly shared on my social media timeline.

Once I started chemo, the realisation that I wasn't superhuman tossed a little more stock in that boiling stew. Nobody – nobody – is ever prepared for chemo. It doesn't matter how many information sessions you attend or how many people you know who've had chemo; the way your body reacts is unique.

"Yes, I will keep coming to my PT sessions," I'd said to my personal trainer. "We may need to modify things a little once I start chemo but there's no reason why I can't keep coming."

Wrong.

The first session I had, a few days after my first chemotherapy infusion,

I nearly passed out. I was sure I was going to spew. My body felt like it had been dragged ten kilometres along a dirt road by a rampaging bull.

That was after the first five minutes. Five. Minutes.

This was bullshit!

And so, I gave up. If I couldn't last five minutes, what was the point?

At least I had dragon boating.

"Make sure you keep coming out in the boat," my dragon boating buddies said. "Even if you just sit at the front and come along for the ride."

"Great," I'd said with genuine enthusiasm and intent. That was pre-chemo. It was also pre my epic fail at the gym.

So, I dropped that as well. I'd take my daughter along to training and I'd sit in the car and wait to take her home again three times a week. I didn't mind that so much; it was a good opportunity for time alone with a book. Sometimes one of the team would pick her up instead or bring her home at the end of the training session, but it was often me at first. It was all part of the 'I must be independent' attitude.

The worst thing about doing this was watching the boat pull out at the start of the session. I'd sit and watch them load the boat, get settled, ready-to-backset – they'd reverse-paddle out, turn and disappear through the mouth of the bay and out of sight.

You have no idea how hard that is, to watch when all you want is to be in the boat with them. The first few times, I was genuinely upset – near tears upset. That should be me, I'd think. Often I'd rage at the unfairness of it all. A 'kick the gravel and stub your toe' type of rage that makes you look and feel like a toddler in the midst of a tantrum.

Eventually, I stopped watching. I just couldn't.

I actually felt a white-hot hatred for them – those who could, when I couldn't.

I knew the anger I was feeling was irrational; a coping mechanism. It was a façade to hide behind in the same way Denial and Shock had been. Anything was better than facing the truth, the fear and the pain.

Yet, still, Anger dipped and rose. Swirled and danced. Weaved her way into every situation.

I angered at those who failed to hold doors open for me. And at those who did.

I angered at those who said I looked well when I felt like shit; those who cast sympathetic glances and insisted on holding my elbow or patting my arm when I felt good.

I angered at my lack of strength and my resilience that made me tired.

And I angered at my angering.

"Atta girl," said Cancer, with the smirk of the ultimate manipulator.

"Shut up," I'd yell. Angry. "Fuck the hell off!"

Most of all, I angered at Cancer. She'd turned me into someone I wasn't. Someone I didn't want to be.

The way anger sounds

By all means, get mad, throw a few vases, yell and scream
"I'm sick of this stupid cancer!" – but then move on.
There's more to life.

~ Katherine ~

My daughter was furious.
"Why are you waiting so long?" she said.

The surgery date was out of my hands
and she knew that, but still …

~ Elly ~

"Look," I said when I got in to see her,
"we need to do something about these cysty boobs.
I can't bear this anymore.
There must be something we can do.
This is painful."

~ Natalie ~

It was not a time for being stubborn, nor was it a time to transform into a helpless invalid; it was a time that called for determination that acknowledged my inner strength as well as my limitations.

Determination

n. a mental attitude characterized by a strong commitment to achieving a particular goal despite barriers and hardships.

Fifteen years prior to the year my life took an uncharted path, I had found myself visiting a naturopath of sorts. She was an older lady, but not old. Her place was located in a squeezy corner store at a local shopping centre, flanked by a butcher shop and across the way from the hairdressing salon I used to go to as a teenager. A darkened room lay beyond the doorway, walls lined with small brown bottles and packets of different colours with Chinese script. A large chart on the back wall showed a series of images of the iris – not the flower, but the coloured part of your eye. The chart also showed the inner workings of the eyeball, diagrams that caused me to find elsewhere to look as cross-section images of eyes have always made my own squint and water.

Had I been harnessing the overactive and stereotyped imagination of my inner child, I would have immediately connected this naturopath with what I knew of witches. It was all the potions and icky pictures. Yet, the lady herself was far from wicked.

She smiled as I entered. "Welcome. You must be Kellie. Take a seat. I shan't be long."

On closer inspection, she had no chin warts sprouting hair and, as far as I could see into the dark corners of her shop, there was no bubbling cauldron. My nose did not detect a cat of any sort, black or otherwise.

I had made this appointment on the recommendation of a friend, who herself had been under the lady's care for a while with a good level of success.

Women's issues.

The curse.

The 'P' word.

For goodness sake! Once you've birthed a baby or suffered the indignity of a pap smear or breast pummelling – otherwise referred to as a mammogram – all sense of shame and embarrassment is merely relative, so I'm going to say it out loud and in full: I was here in the hope she could sort out my periods. Those inconvenient yet highly necessary occurrences had, for me, from day one, only been regular in their irregularity. They'd been controlled by the pill for longer than I could remember.

Too long, as it turns out.

Oh, the joy of hindsight.

She motioned me towards a stool, one leg of which wobbled with an unsatisfying wonkiness as I positioned myself, taking great care not to sit off-centre or too heavily.

I looked up and found her staring – with what turned out to be a lengthy and uncomfortable intensity – directly into my eyes.

"Silk eye," she said.

"Pardon?" Had I heard correctly? Silk … eye? It sounded less than good – like cataracts but perhaps worse. My husband had been fascinated by a documentary on television that showed a cataract operation. I couldn't watch it – a quick glance up from my book had made my eyes water.

"Iridology," she said. "You have a silk constitution. Basically, you've got strong genetic material. You're less prone to disease."

I wasn't sure what this had to do with my periods, but I was nonetheless interested. "So, I won't get sick?" This bit I didn't really believe because I'd had a childhood filled with colds and tonsilitis. Then again, as far as I knew, I'd managed to avoid the childhood nasties of chicken pox and mumps.

"I didn't say that." She selected a brown bottle off the shelf and held it out. "A quarter teaspoon before food, twice a day. It doesn't taste pleasant but if you persevere it will regulate your cycle within about two months."

The bottle was labelled with more Chinese script but also had the instructions she'd just given me handwritten in English underneath. I took the bottle, unscrewed the lid and gagged. "And the silk eye?"

"Oh, yes. You can still get sick but your body will fight it off more effectively."

I thought of my grandmother. All the illnesses she'd had over the years and she was still with us. "Is it genetic?" I asked as I handed over what seemed to be an obscene amount of money for a few hundred millilitres of stagnant pond sludge.

She nodded and pocketed my cash. "Yes," she said. "Like eye colour."

That conversation came back to me as I sat in the cubicle at the imaging centre, naked but for my undies and one of those front-opening smocks that are not made for anybody with proper boobs. I was waiting to be called in for yet another scan. I'd lost count of how many I'd had, but this one required a cannula and an injection of some sort of dye.

"Don't be stupid," said Cancer. "Surely you don't believe in that hippy voodoo iridology guff? I thought you were more sensible than that."

"Scared, are you?" I asked.

Cancer snorted. "Yeah, right," she huffed.

I narrowed my silk eyes in Cancer's direction and stared without blinking.

Cancer was the first to look away.

I was one was of those 'well-cooked' babies. Refused to come on my due date. Or the week after. My mother had been advised to drink castor oil to hasten me along. Apparently the stuff tastes vile, plus it's now recommended for constipation. Mum drank it. I'm not sure if it worked or not but I'm here now.

Castor oil or not, I came when I was ready and that attitude is how I live my life.

"You can't change her mind," Mum often says of me, or words to that effect.

It is, I know, a source of frustration to her. We are alike in more ways than either of us care to admit.

I was born stubborn and I own it. One hundred per cent.

If I stuff up or miss out on something, it's on me. I prefer it that way. It's much better to blame myself for something than resent someone else for their perceived inadequacy. It's not like I don't want to try new ways or different approaches to doing things, but I want it to be in my own time, on my terms.

Part of this attitude has to do with this fear of failure thing I've had going since … forever. Being scared of failing is not a good thing. In fact, my fear of failure stopped me from doing a lot of things in my childhood, like running for house captain in Year 6 and trying out for the extension class in high school. It can be debilitating if left unchecked.

Along life's travels I must have learned to harness this fear, though, because at some point in my early-to-mid-twenties I found myself striving to do things I'd have shied away from in the past. Things like applying for a scholarship to study in Japan for a year, putting my hand up to be president of the Japanese Language Teachers' Association, mentoring pre-service teachers and, more recently, volunteering to read out my writing at workshops.

That fear was still there but I moulded it into a cannonball. If I couldn't face failing, then I simply wouldn't allow myself to fail.

Dogged, obstinate, blinkered stubbornness.

I don't necessarily recommend it because, shit, the stubborn life is a tough way to live!

It's funny, when you think about it, how different words essentially mean the same thing but have completely opposite nuances.

Take 'stubborn' and 'determined' for example. There is nothing good about being called stubborn and having this tendency as one of your identified personality traits. Being stubborn implies that you'll be hard to work with, not a team player, difficult to get along with, inflexible.

On the other hand, 'determination' is a trait worthy of accolades.

"You're determined not to let this cancer beat you," someone said to me when I insisted on accompanying my daughter to dragon boating nationals and then holding my team's drink bottles and assorted paraphernalia as they filed past me, boarding the boat for their next race.

"That's good," the same person added. "Positivity can go a long way."

True. I don't disagree with the power of positive thinking, but at the time I honestly thought I was just being stubborn. I hadn't really wanted to go to nationals. I certainly didn't want to watch my team race when I wanted to be on the water with them. It was devastating seeing them load, reverse back and start heading to the start line. But I was buggered if I was going to show anybody that, so I pushed through despite feeling like crap, despite being miserable that I was missing out, despite feeling like the third wheel or the mascot.

Stubborn, or determined?

Same thing, really.

My determination phase hit very early. In fact, Determination joined the party only a couple of days after I'd seen the surgeon and had sort of come to terms with what I was facing.

"Get the fuck out of my way, Denial and Shock, I've got work to do." Determination was the master of the 'teacher eye' – the glare that can pull students into line without lifting a finger or whispering a word. It's a stare full of menace and 'try-me' attitude. "Anger, you can hang around. Occasionally you come in handy."

Determination had things sorted.

First task – request extended leave. Tick.

Second task – make some firm decisions about what I would and wouldn't do or accept in terms of 'help'. Not medical help, as I'd already decided to go with the experts, but help from family, friends and colleagues.

I considered what I'd already been offered, ticking items off mentally.

Meals? These were offered by random friends and my teaching colleagues on a roster. Yes – but not every night.

Transport to and from chemo and other associated appointments? My mother, my husband and a colleague who was on leave herself all offered this service. No, thank you – unless I was physically unable to get myself there. And that wasn't going to happen if I could help it.

A lift for my daughter to and from dragon boating and the gym? This was kindly offered by various teammates and a friend who we shared gym sessions with. No, I could still drive. Not an issue.

Company during the six-hour chemo sessions? Hell no! There is no better time to catch up on one's reading than when you have a needle in your arm with poison seeping into your body. What on earth would I find to talk about for six hours anyway?

Shopping? Already done online so not needed.

House-cleaning? Nobody offered to do that. It's the one thing I would've jumped at too.

On the whole, though, I was determined. Stubborn. Whatever you want to call it. No help. I had cancer. I was not bedridden, nor had I lost limbs or my marbles.

I had this.

As the days moved on and I got further into the shittiness of chemo, I began to figure out the difference between being stubborn and being determined.

Stubborn is when you stick to your guns, no matter what – even if it's to your detriment.

Determined is when you stick to your guns but have enough nous to know when to adjust the parameters a little to accommodate changes in circumstance.

I learned to swallow that pride and say 'yes' to offers from teammates to transport my daughter to and from dragon boat training. "We're totally out of your way," I argued at first. "We can't let you do that."

One friend put things back into perspective for me, though. "I don't drive Fred Flintstone's car, you know," she retorted.

Pride swallowed, I graciously – and increasingly gratefully – accepted the offers.

Occasionally, I allowed a friend to pick me up and drive me to gatherings or social events – never appointments, though. I relished those chemo sessions for the peace and largely uninterrupted reading time they gave me. And the house-cleaning? Well, let's just say nobody ever died from sleeping in an unmade bed … although the sunlight catching on the dust sheen and making it sparkle was a bit annoying.

"Don't ever let anybody tell you what to do or how to feel. Nobody knows what you're going through, except you. Take the advice you want and tell the rest to fuck off."

I've forgotten exactly who said that to me. It was someone from my dragon boating club, I know that much. Someone who'd already travelled a road similar to the one I was on. The words stuck with me and forced me to listen to my body.

The ability to harness my determination and maintain it came from internal strength, conviction and, yes, stubbornness, as well as from several external sources.

Having breast cancer was like being in a new, exclusive club – one you could only join if you've had a parasitic invader stake its claim on one or both of your breasts. Of course, there were plenty of 'non-members' who were there for me as well, and these people cannot go unacknowledged. But, the ladies who'd been through what I was about to go through – my fellow dragon boaters, colleagues, friends – became special in an understated way I cannot adequately describe in words. They 'got it'. And just knowing that, knowing they'd pulled through it all, was enough to give power to my determination.

Other factors weighed in with significant input into this phase – my writing, my kids, my personal trainer, my grandmother and a particular friend who I deeply admire.

Sometimes I think that writing saved me – or at least stopped me from going totally nuts. I wrote every day of my leave. Not about cancer as you might assume. Not journal entries, although I did receive a very nice journal from the Breast Cancer Network of Australia. I never once wrote in it. Instead, I started a blog and wrote ramblings about quotes I found – my take on them and what resonated with me in that moment. Sometimes they turned into a rant about chemo … but other times they were a reflection about something else entirely. I was also determined to keep up my writing sessions with my mentor and writing buddy – I had a novel to work on, and although I can't say I honestly got too far with it, just having it there to distract me from feeling sorry for myself did wonders.

It was a sense of normality that kept me going.

Maintaining a routine was also incredibly important – not for me, per se, but for my kids. A huge part of my determination stemmed from my need to disrupt their lives as little as I could. They were in Year 8 and Year 6 at the time – not really the most stable ages to weather disruption. Good teachers and supportive friends helped maintain their sense of normality, offering support only when it was asked for.

My grandmother was key to my determination, as was my friend and teaching colleague, Janet. Both of these ladies had refused to succumb to cancer in its different forms. Both stood tall as remarkable, compassionate and modest women who I aspired to be like. I didn't want to disappoint either of them. I was inspired by Janet's wisdom and calm strength and her catchphrase, 'Carpe Diem'. And I was buggered if I was going to let Cancer win and leave my grandmother with unwarranted guilt.

Determination, buoyed by wonderful, inspiring people, was key to my progress. I firmly believe that. However, I'm also going to hold Determination responsible for a few setbacks.

Cancer laughed at me on the day of my first chemo treatment. "I've grown. I'm in your lymph nodes. Come on – what's the point?"

I saw this laughter for what it was – typical bully bravado. But, like all who have been bullied in this way, a little worm of doubt still niggled. It edged its way in and took up space, working its little butt off to drain my resolve.

With a smug smile, Cancer sat with me while I waited in the recliner chair, water bottle and book in easy reach, trying not to stare at the other patients.

"Are you ready?" asked the chemo nurse, one of the angels of this ward.

"Absolutely," I said. My voice wavered slightly. Was I ready? What was going to happen? Was there any point?

Cancer snickered.

"Tell her to fuck off," Determination whispered.

I took a deep breath. "Fuck the hell off," I said. The chemo nurse widened his eyes. "Not you," I added. "Cancer."

He nodded. He'd heard it all before – and probably worse.

"Awww," Cancer whined. Her voice dripped with fake disappointment and insincere distress. "I thought the two of us really had something there. In it together, you know?"

Swallowing my trepidation, I allowed Determination to take the floor. "Shove that needle in and let's set about destroying this sucker," I said.

It worked.

As the first wash of saline flowed cold through my veins, I felt Cancer's resolve deflate just a smidge. The thought of that silk eye, the whisper of 'Carpe Diem' and, above all, my grandmother's strength warmed my body and eased my mind.

The way determination sounds

"Right now," my oncologist said, "you're around eighty per cent chance of no recurrence. Chemo would maybe bring it to ninety-two."

I had a fourteen-month-old child who I wanted to be around for. "I think I'm a ninety-two sort of girl," I said. "I'm a high achiever. I think I would like the chemo."

I also knew what I was getting into. I'd been there before.

~ Che ~

The mastectomy went really well. So much so, I went to the movies the day I got out of hospital. My family were going to see *Mamma Mia* and I just said, "You're not going without me."

They protested, of course, but I failed to see why I couldn't go. I was fine. There'd been no complications and I wasn't in pain. Sure, I had a drain in, but nothing else. "I'm coming," I said, and that was it.

~ Gillian ~

I owned it [the baldness]. It made me feel I could deal with everything and that I was making the best of it all. Actually, I became a bit theatrical with the head gear. I had the most beautiful scarves and I'd wear them with boldness. I'd have great big earrings and big bright tops and bright yellow pants. The way I saw it was that I didn't want to lock myself away, saying, "Oh, poor me."

~ Joanne ~

After a while, I'd move out into the loungeroom and cover myself with a blanket. I liked being there with them. I'd try to play when I could – you still have to be a mum, even when you're sick.

~ Sugar ~

As if I'd inadvertently sucked on an astringent persimmon, the set of my mouth heralded the onset of hostility and a sense that nothing would ever be right in my world again.

Hostility

__n.__ the overt expression of intense animosity or antagonism in action, feeling, or attitude.

If I was asked to describe Calvary Hospital in two words, it would be hills and stairs. What this meant was a full cardio workout every time I went for a chemo session, a blood test or an appointment with my oncologist. Weekly, in other words, if not twice-weekly.

The wheeze and the red face and the huff and puff were embarrassing. At least the red face gave my normal corpse-like pallor some colour, but still – not nice. "Give me a second," I'd pant whenever I finally reached the reception desk, struggling to get four words out, let alone who I was, who I was seeing and when my appointment was.

I'd hear Cancer snicker but lacked the energy to slap that snickery-smirk off her smug face. It was Determination's fault anyway, Anger reminded me.

She was right. "Have to do it yourself," Determination always urged. "You're independent; no need to have someone drop you at the door. You're determined, remember!"

It was all forgotten once I'd finished the appointment, looking forward to the downhill meander back to my car and the quick drive home where a snack might await me – reward for my toils.

"Look at you, standing there," said Cancer. "Can't walk up a little hill without coming over all old and wheezy. You can't even look at yourself in the mirror." Cancer started up with her needling every time she saw a gap in my will. The slightest indication of a downer. A sigh.

"Whatever," I said, without meaning it. My head was prickling with beaded sweat. Stupid headwear. Inside, I was comprised of shards of ice. I pulled open the second-top drawer of my tallboy – it smelled of mothballs even though I'd never bought a mothball in my life – and pulled out a clean pair of leggings. Checked for holes. There were none.

"You eat shit and your body shows it," Cancer sneered.

Hostility chimed in. "Bet you wish chemo made you spew and lose your appetite like it does for most people." Her words were always razor-sharp. They cut with a surgeon's precision. "Alternatively, you could harness this thing called self-control."

Other people. The ones for whom nausea was a relentless companion for the duration of their treatment and beyond. Who couldn't eat. Who lost an unhealthy amount of weight they could ill afford to lose as their bodies struggled to combat the poison. I should be grateful I didn't have that side effect; grateful that I didn't need the anti-nausea tablets sitting unopened in my bathroom cabinet. But sometimes I wasn't. Can you even believe that?

Hostility nudged me with her elbow as I side-eyed my appearance in the mirror. I pushed her away – how dare she! Who was I to be jealous of others who were sicker than I was; who had it so much worse than me?

Cancer's voice grew stronger with each word as she followed me down the hall and into the kitchen. "Go on," she said. "Eat while you can. You'll never know when a meal may be your last. Besides, there's no point worrying about what you look like … not right now. No hair. Dry skin. No colour …" She knew my weak spots. She saw exactly where to strike.

"Go away," I said. I took the last biscuit from the tin. Took a bite. I may as well have eaten the packet. Cardboard.

Almost everything I put in my mouth tasted the same – metallic, with stale water-cracker overtones. Citrus was good, though. The more lemony the better. As for everything else, it was like eating silken tofu straight from the packet – on its own. Not even a dash of soy sauce and a few bonito flakes. I used to quite like the 'nothing' flavour of tofu … when I had tastebuds that worked and I'd tired of overly sauced and spiced foods.

You always covet what you don't have.

Quarter to ten. I'd need to leave in five minutes to give myself enough time.

I stood in front of the bathroom mirror and adjusted my headwear. It may as well have been a clown hat with flashing lights and a sign that read *Cancer Victim – no hair; regrets not getting a wig!*

I had a couple of different cotton skull caps. A plain black one I tried to accessorise with a red or blue scarf. A flowery, blush pink one that I would never have chosen at any other time. And a bluey-grey-black one. I rotated them around with a small selection of clothes – black leggings, oversized t-shirts, two jumpers. The joys of being at home all the time. Barely the next step up from pyjamas.

On this particular day, I had to look half-presentable because I was attending a meeting at my son's school. Already annoyed that I even had to go, nothing I wore was going to satisfy me so I snarled at the mirror and stepped away. My reflection shrugged at me, uncaring.

The school was a ten-minute walk away. The weather was pleasant; warm but not hot. The leaves underfoot, nice and crunchy. I was in my good week – the seven days prior to my next chemo session. "I'll walk down," I said aloud for accountability purposes. Just needed my keys. It would be several hours before anyone else was home and I didn't fancy sitting out on the back verandah until then. They were probably in the kitchen.

"Pah," said Cancer. "Reckon you'll make it?"

"Yes," I said.

No keys on the kitchen bench. Backtrack, Kellie. When did you last use them?

"Red-faced and huffing …" Cancer was clearly not done mocking me for the day.

Where were my keys?

The clock ticked, an ominous tone – late, late, late.

I shook my bag. A familiar jingle told me they were in there … somewhere. I rummaged around, my fingers found unused tissues and pushed aside an old Ventolin puffer that had long ago run out of puff. Ha! Cold metal. Gotcha.

"… a shuffling corpse …"

The useless Ventolin puffer left my fingers and flew across the room. Bloody Cancer saw it coming. "One day," I threatened.

She smirked.

Skittering feet followed me to the front entrance, eager and puppy-like. Hostility, Determination, Anger … ready for an outing.

"Not you," I said as Anger sidled up beside me. "I already have a reputation as 'that' parent at the school. I don't need you making it worse." I grabbed Determination's hand and slipped out before the others could follow, locking the door behind me.

Anger tapped on the glass of the side window, her face pressed against it, fuming at the injustice of being left behind. Peeking out from behind Anger was Self-Pity; she was an offspring of Hostility and I refused to acknowledge her or get to know her beyond the occasional cursory greeting. I heard her sniffle and saw the tears well.

Determination tugged me away and together we blew raspberries at Cancer the whole way to the school. We arrived right on time and only slightly red of face.

The school psychologist was late. That was her first mistake – leaving me sitting in the front foyer on a wooden bench outside the deputy principal's office like a kid who'd been sent to third-stage time out.

Pride and Self-Consciousness rallied together to make me pretend to be busy on my phone as people wandered past. Eventually, a good fifteen minutes after our arranged time, a pair of green-stockinged legs in sensible shoes stopped in front of my downcast gaze.

I hadn't met the school psychologist before, though I knew her name from emails and matched it with the badge she wore, pinned crooked to her chest.

"Kellie?" she said and introduced herself. "Sorry I'm running a little late – so busy at the moment."

"Aren't we all," I muttered, even though 'we' weren't.

She smiled at me, broad and patronising. "This way." The school psychologist pointed down the corridor towards the Kindy classrooms. She took hold of my elbow.

I'll say that again.

She took hold of my elbow.

I sidestepped away, pulling out of her reach. "I'm fine," I said.

"It's okay." She reached for my elbow again. How stupid was this woman? "You look a little pale, that's all." She gestured at my head as I glared her down.

You would think a psychologist would be skilled in reading reactions.

"I don't need help to walk down the corridor," I said. "But thank you."

A lack of hair does not render one's legs useless – that's what I wanted to say. The words were strong and clear in my mind. But I didn't say them.

At least, I thought I didn't say them aloud.

The look on her face suggested otherwise.

"Okay," she said. She walked carefully, baby steps, alongside me.

For a moment I felt sorry for this woman. You're an ungrateful cow, I thought. So inconsiderate.

I checked behind me, thinking perhaps Anger had followed me here after all. She was nowhere to be seen, but I realised I'd neglected to check where Hostility was lurking and make sure she was locked up safe with Anger and Self-Pity before I left.

"Over there," Determination nodded towards the pulsing yellow glow hiding under the bench I'd just been sitting on. "Control her."

"Too late," I said.

Cancer clapped her hands with glee and beckoned Hostility her way. "I'd rather have had Anger by my side, but you'll do in a pinch," she said.

Hostility smiled at me; not a pleasant 'I've got your back' smile, but an 'I told you so and now you'll have to pay' smile. I shouldn't have come. I should have insisted on a phone call. I felt like shit. I looked like shit. I didn't even know what this meeting was for.

Determination poked me in the ribs. "Give it a rest," she said. "You're a teacher. You know the drill."

She was right. Her words made me stand taller and stride down the corridor. My legs were tired but not enough to need a chaperone. The school psychologist had made an assumption based on what I was wearing on my head. I'd pinged her for it. End of story. I brushed away the last of my regret at how I'd reacted.

The meeting turned out to be a hand-holding session in which I was required to fill in a long questionnaire regarding my son's transition to high school. It was standard practice for the Intervention Support Program and was a form I'd completed countless times before, both as a teacher and a parent.

Hostility cleared her throat.

"Why didn't you send this home so I could fill it in there?" I asked, stabbing the next response onto the page with my pen.

"I thought you might need some help," she said.

Having no hair does not render one's brain dead, I thought – taking great care to keep my mouth closed.

"But you know I'm a teacher, right?" It took everything I had to keep my tone light. The poker face and the poker voice are not skills I possess. "And that he's in Year 6, so I've actually completed this exact same form before." I sighed – loud and exaggerated. "Twice, actually."

"Well, yes ..." The psychologist's gaze fluttered once again to my headwear and I stared at her till she looked elsewhere. The teacher eye works just as effectively on adults. "I just thought ... you know ... you might appreciate the support."

The words I'd previously thought – about the assumptions people make when you're mid-treatment and shiny-scalped – pushed their way out of my mouth and clattered noisily around the room, bouncing off the walls in their joy at being free. "Just because I have cancer," I said, pronouncing every word with precise care, "does not render me totally incompetent."

Her mouth gaped like a fish.

I did not apologise.

But neither did she.

I completed the form – by myself – and left without further incident. An hour of my life I wasn't getting back.

The ten-minute walk home took twenty. My head hurt. My legs ached. My face felt red, bloated and itchy. And I was thirsty. I peeled my tongue off the roof of my mouth like Velcro and licked my lips. "What a bloody waste of time," I muttered. "Psychologist, my arse."

"Ugh." Determination pranced off in disgust, leaving me to walk alone with Cancer's pompous tone in my head.

"That form took you a lot longer to fill in than it should have," Cancer said. "You haven't been thinking straight of late. Wake up to yourself and accept it. You know what's going on – just admit it."

"I'll admit nothing to you," I said. I fumbled with the key. The lock was sticking, and after loosening it with a few choice words I wrenched the door open.

Self-Pity leapt into my arms and, for once, I allowed her to snuggle into my chest. It only lasted a minute before she was smacked away by Hostility, who'd been breathing down my neck the whole way home, waiting to have her say.

She left nothing in her tank as she berated me for my lack of control. "You just can't do it, can you," she said, lip curled in disgust. "You clearly can't be bothered to even try and retain some of your dignity." Shades of self-hatred.

I tore off my headwear and, feeling the prickle of unheated air on my naked scalp, tossed the stupid piece of cloth up the hall. I wanted to cry. To curl up and bawl like a baby. But I was unable to squeeze even one salty tear from my stinging eyes as I was too dehydrated from neglecting to take a bottle of water with me on that hot and sweaty walk.

Hostility was, to be frank, more than a little draining. Indeed, she sucked more life and energy out of me than my chemo sessions or walks up the hill did. It may have been because, for the most part, I tried to keep Hostility contained; an inward emotion. Of course, she slipped out at the most unfortunate times – usually teaming up with Anger. She didn't appreciate her containment and chose instead to eat away at me from the inside.

Like me, Hostility wore a number of metaphorical hats – a different one each time she paid a visit. The hats ranged from awkwardness and embarrassment to shame, disgust and resentful sorrow.

The old chestnut of 'why me?' didn't appear too often. That was largely thanks to the people – other patients – I saw at Zita Mary Clinic. They were all much worse off than me. And even if they weren't, they seemed to be.

It was more the escalation of my lifelong self-consciousness and fears of what other people thought about me that filled Hostility's bucket. This wasn't helped by the naïve and occasionally insensitive reactions of those around me.

Hostility was really like a naughty puppy. She slept quite a bit, but when awake she'd tangle herself around my feet and trip me over, leaving me to fall flat on my face if I wasn't paying attention.

Also like a puppy, though, Hostility could be trained. Most of the time, she walked attentively by my side – albeit on a leash – occasionally becoming distracted by the sight of another of her kind or an intriguing smell in the long grass.

I have never enjoyed being the centre of attention and I missed my anonymity. It had been stolen by Cancer and replaced by the flashing lights of a plastic pallor, hairless façade and what I can only describe as an aura of unwellness that made people either open doors for me or avoid my gaze and general proximity.

The times I felt this most were the times I was drawn into Hostility's sticky web. It took every shred of my stubborn Determination to free myself from her hold.

"I'm so pleased with your progress," my oncologist announced as he waited for me to struggle back into my clothes. "How many do you have left?"

"One," I said, knowing he was referring to my schedule of chemo sessions and not my breasts. I still had two of them ... for now.

"Excellent. Let's talk about Herceptin then."

I nodded. I had no idea what that was, though I'm sure he'd mentioned it in the past.

"You can have it intravenously," he said, "or through injection."

I blanched. Intravenous meant more cannulas and more digging around trying to find a vein in my veinless arms.

The first couple of chemo treatments had been fine. The nurse had managed to find a vein on the second or third go. It had brought back memories of my father and his bruised, pinpricked arms each time he'd been hospitalised for asthma and worse. "I hope you don't get my veins," he used to say to me. Sorry, Dad – I most certainly did.

The next couple of treatments, my veins got cluey, sinking low and tightening up – necessitating a copious consumption of water, along with heat packs, warm blankets and squeezy balls to coax them to the surface, ready to be speared.

However, the most recent venture had been nothing short of a debacle.

Those poor nurses.

There were three of them on duty. I went through them all. Three tries and you're out – that was the rule among the chemo nurses at Zita Mary.

It meant they only had three goes to get the cannula in before having to pass my pincushion arm over to someone else.

It left them no option but to resort to the ultrasound machine – and even that required much digging and swearing … from all of us.

My arm had been a mess. Today, I can still close my eyes and feel the needle moving around in my arm as the nurse tries and fails, tries and fails, to pierce the vein.

Bringing myself back to the oncologist's office, a familiar tug in my gut pre-empted the tight throat and salty eyes, heralding the arrival of Self-Pity. She enveloped me in a limp hug. It wasn't fair.

I winced as Hostility pushed Self-Pity away.

No, I thought. Bugger this. I took a deep breath and shoved both of them away, closing the lid on their box to let them sort each other out away from me. Determination sat on the lid, keeping them contained and swinging her legs. She smiled with a certain smugness that I found instantly satisfying.

"Is one better than the other?" I asked.

My oncologist opened his mouth to answer but I cut him off.

"Only – I really, really want to avoid intravenous if I can …"

He nodded. "It's much the same, although those injections can really hurt. Really, really hurt. It goes straight into your thigh muscle."

Ha-ha. Hurt? Really hurt! Whatever. A bit of hurt, I could manage. They could come at me with a needle the thickness of my finger and I'd scoff at it. Being prodded and dug at for half an hour – that, I couldn't do.

"Injection," I said.

My oncologist nodded. "I think we can organise that."

As I walked back out to my car – thankful it was parked at the bottom of the hill – Cancer cleared her throat.

"What now?" I said. I cracked open the lid of the box, allowing Hostility room to breathe and hoping she'd return the favour.

"You haven't won yet," Cancer croaked. "That oncologist you admire so much – he's paid to make you feel positive."

"He's also paid to be my hitman," I said.

It felt good to say that out loud and know it was true. Know we were winning. I thanked Hostility for channelling her narkiness to help me out for a change.

"Hmmph," Cancer said and then added … nothing.

The way hostility sounds

Every time I watched TV, all I saw were voluptuous women
with their boobs hanging out. It wasn't fair –
I was going to be losing mine soon and I had to
watch these people flaunting themselves.

~ Clare ~

The other thing that played on my mind was the time delay between having a negative result and going back for the mammogram. A voice in my head was saying, "If you'd hurried, if you'd got to it more quickly, maybe it might have been different."

~ Anne ~

Wallowing in one's guilt is not unlike sneaking that last piece of chocolate cake and savouring it, bite by greedy bite, then swallowing the last crumbs with remorse and a promise to make amends.

Guilt

__n.__ a self-conscious emotion characterized by a painful appraisal of having done (or thought) something that is wrong and often by a readiness to take action designed to undo or mitigate this wrong.

Guilt is irrational.

She's an energy suck. Her purpose is to deflect other, less savoury thoughts about pain, dying and death but, in doing so, she replaces these thoughts with ones that beat you down and have you believe that everything said and done is your fault.

Guilt is the most sly of emotions. She loiters along busy streets in a heavy coat fitted with pockets of varying sizes. Each pocket contains a slip of paper upon which is written a single word or phrase. This word may be construed as an instruction – or perhaps even a prophesy – that pertains to the source of guilt: colleagues, children, friends, people who are sicker than you, your own inner turmoil, or even your self-loathing.

Guilt hands these slips out to passers-by, peddling her wares.

Some take the slips and read them as they walk. They veer off track and stumble over unsuspecting pedestrians or into the paths of oncoming bicycles or stationary poles.

Others take the slip out of courtesy and stuff it into the pocket of their jeans or into their handbag, along with all their receipts and used tissues.

Many people take the slip, before surreptitiously crumpling it and tossing it in the closest bin or perhaps behind them, as if by accident. "Oops! How did that slip from my hand? Oh dear! Where did it go?" Either way, whether binned or littered, the slip unfurls itself from its crumpled state and lifts its arms to the breeze. Duly caught, it flutters and swirls, following the recipient. It bounces along, at times catching flat against a leg or unmoving object but, persistent, it loosens and continues on. Finally it finds its mark, lodging itself firmly on the bottom of a shoe or gliding neatly into the waiting embrace of a tote bag or hood.

A few people simply ignore the reaching hand of Guilt – they dismiss it as unworthy, a being of lower status. They push past, shaking their head, averting their gaze. "No. Not today, thanks," they mutter. As they pass by, Guilt watches them. Ever patient, Guilt bides her time, knowing she will come to all.

Eventually.

And at a time when it is least expected.

I failed at breastfeeding. Both times. It wasn't through lack of perseverance. Who knows what it was – too big, wrong shape, anxiety on my part, that fear of failure? As a new mum, there's little worse than a hungry baby who's not putting on weight because they're not being fed … and consequently crying all the time and only sleeping for short bursts.

Even now, nearly twenty years after the non-event, that inability to breastfeed still makes me feel incredibly sad. And tired. And inadequate. The words 'you're such a bad mum' play on a never-ending loop like the documentaries at a museum – the ones where you only need to press a button to have them play over again.

The first time round, I persisted with the actual feeding until, one day, it looked like my daughter had been drinking milky tomato juice. Then I switched to expressing for a good four months or so, before fatigue took over and I gave up.

"Don't worry, you did your best," the child health nurse told me as she shook her head; her mouth sympathetic while her eyes radiated disapproval. "Just express, instead; as much as you can. Give her the best chance possible."

So I expressed. For months. Like a cow, I was hooked to my own personal milking machine for hours every day.

The second time round, I was a little more successful but only marginally. He struggled. And so did I until I finally broke.

"I'll go down and get some formula," my husband said for what seemed like the umpteenth time. I'd resisted and resisted. 'Breast is best'. I couldn't fail a second time.

"Do it," I said, then cried and cried until he came home, made it up and handed me the bottle. My baby boy slept for more than two hours for the first time since birth. There was no way I was going back.

Again, disapproval. "Are you sure you don't want to express?" the nurse said. "It's really worth it."

She may as well have told me I'd ruined his life, I thought. If I hadn't been so tired and overwhelmed, I may have said it aloud. Besides, I didn't need any of the 'breast is best' club members bringing me down because I was already doing that quite effectively myself.

Did I miss that bonding opportunity? Had I exposed my kids to childhood illnesses, health issues and lower immunity? Did they miss the nutrition they needed to grow and develop?

Was I a bad mum?

Stupid breasts!

'Mummy-guilt' should be a medical or psychological term. Maybe it is. I'm quite sure it's instigated or exacerbated – or both – by all the parenting books, magazines, blog posts, TV shows and podcasts out there. 'How to be a good parent'. 'How to raise great kids'. 'You can have it all and still be perfect', yada, yada, yada. Couple these with the well-meaning – or sociopathic; take your pick – souls who start their sentences with "Well, my child didn't …" or "When little Frankie was a baby, I never …" and you have yourself a finely-tuned recipe for mummy-guilt.

Why are we never good enough as parents in our own minds? Why can we always 'have done better'? Mummy-guilt starts the second you see that second line on the pregnancy test and ends … never.

With my diagnosis, I was propelled back a decade and a bit to the breastfeeding fiasco, courtesy of a seemingly innocent question from someone.

"Did you breastfeed?" she asked, eyes wide in query.

"What?" I said. "No, I didn't. And that's relevant how?"

"Well," the innocent tone suddenly turned more accusatory, "you know that breastfeeding reduces the risk of breast cancer?"

It's funny – not – how those 'breast is best' radicals lay in wait for the right moment to pounce and say, "I told you so."

I may have told her to fuck right off with her judgements, I'm not sure. If I didn't, I certainly should have. But … the door had been opened.

"This was your fault all along," Guilt cried out. "If only you'd stuck at it longer, you wouldn't be here now, would you!"

She wouldn't let it go, either. And Guilt won't be told to fuck right off because she has the invisible stickiness of a spider's web – the sort you walk through without seeing and then can't get rid of no matter how much you prance about, arms flailing.

Anyway, here's the thing: that lifetime of mummy-guilt we all experience is nothing – I repeat, nothing – compared to mummy-guilt plus mummy-has-cancer-guilt.

This combination is totally next level. Not only do you have the normal mummy-guilt things to feel bad about, but there's the added joy of feeling even worse because some aspect of your cancer prevents you from doing something with or for your kids.

I exaggerate.

Or do I?

One of the first things I did when I got my diagnosis was email my kids' teachers to let them know.

> *I've just been diagnosed with breast cancer. I'm going to have all the treatment thrown at it – starting with chemotherapy in a couple of weeks. [My child's name] knows and is coping well at the moment.*

> *However, I would appreciate you letting me know if you notice any unusual behaviour or little flags. I will also keep you informed from this end. Please feel free to let other staff know as well, particularly those who know and work with [child].*

I wasn't a fan of dumbing things down and beating around the bush, whether in person or via email. Take it or leave it, at least people didn't have to guess what I was thinking.

I received quite a few emails back, all promising to look out for the relevant child. The primary school email elicited a number of responses from teachers who'd previously taught my son or who knew me as a colleague. The high school – a much less personal response as I didn't know these people – offered support and counselling for my daughter.

About a week later, I had occasion to speak in person to my son's teacher – a young lad, barely out of nappies himself as far as teaching experience went.

"He knows about the breast cancer," I said, looking him straight in the eye. "He seems okay, but just watch him."

The poor man was quite lost for words and didn't know where to place his gaze after I first said the 'B' word and followed it up with the 'C' word – breast cancer.

"What did you say 'cancer' for?" Guilt whispered. "And did you really have to tell him where the cancer was? He's only young. Look how uncomfortable you've made him feel."

"He knew anyway," I whispered back. "It was in the email, remember!"

I sat back in the chair and waited until the teacher looked at me again. I said nothing, so he was forced to.

"I will," he said. "If there's anything I can do …"

"He probably won't say much," I waded on, ignoring the warning shake of Guilt's head. "He won't want to talk about it, but just so you know, my chemo starts in two weeks." Another 'C' word. Both equally as shocking as the uncouth, sweary 'C' word, apparently.

My daughter's school – a high school, and much less welcoming – recommended referring her to the psychologist "… just so she can touch base with your daughter every so often." Great.

That very afternoon: "They pulled me out of class so I could talk about my feelings," my daughter reported the second she walked in the front door.

"And?" I said.

"Yeah," she said. "I don't need to." She was fourteen – the teenage equivalent of the 'terrible twos'.

"Nice one," Guilt said.

"Disrupting her education," Cancer chimed in, clucking her razor tongue in disapproval. "Making her stand out when all she needs is to blend in."

"Wait till they stick that needle in my arm," I retorted. "That'll shut you up."

"And you'll be even more useless to your kids than normal," said Cancer, as if she wasn't remotely concerned about her own future.

Bravado in the face of fear.

We both suffered from it.

Guilt invited herself to stay the second I was diagnosed. She was there for every occasion. Lurked in every corner. Followed me absolutely everywhere I went. She missed nothing.

The house was full of flowers for quite some time after the word got out. No shelf was left un-blossomed. Big bouquets that had to be split between several vases. Arrangements that came in soggy-bottomed boxes with that weird green foamy stuff that needed to be kept damp but not soaking wet, as I discovered to my detriment. Australian natives through to gladiolas and those stinky lilies that protest their imprisonment by releasing a dog fart every half hour or so. So many flowers I had to put some outside.

Guilt.

Chocolates. By the boxload. Why do people give chocolates for every occasion – happy, sad or indifferent? The easy gift. I gave several boxes away.

Guilt.

Care packs containing socks, notebooks, slippers, beanies and heat bags that all smelled of lavender and made me sneeze. I didn't use some of them.

Guilt.

The cards were a mixed bag – some just with a name, others with expressions of everything from the sender's deep sorrow through to the uplifting 'kick cancer's arse' messages. I rather enjoyed the thought that Cancer had no friends – and that I had more than I realised.

Guilt.

Yes, guilt, because I hadn't realised so many people cared. And I felt guilty for ignoring them.

Then, after the flow of flowers and other paraphernalia had slowed down a bit, someone said something like "You truly don't know how many people care about you until something like this happens."

Guiltily, I wondered if that were actually true or if people just came out of the woodwork at times like these because it is the 'right thing to do'.

I arm-wrestled with Guilt constantly. We became stuck in a position where neither of us could summon that last smidge of strength to win.

Guilt and I were in limbo.

"I'm so sorry you've been left with all of this," I'd said to my colleague early on in the term.

We were a team of two and I'd gone and left her to deal with the admin required at the start of the school year. Admin for the two-hundred-or-so kids we were responsible for in our role as ESL teachers. The fact that I had been hit with a swathe of medical appointments was irrelevant in my mind. I truly felt like I'd let her down.

"Are you kidding?" she said. "Why would you feel bad about that?"

Because it sure beats worrying about Cancer and where she's set her sights on next in my body. I thought this. I didn't say it.

Taking all that leave compounded Guilt's hold.

"You don't want to think about it?" Guilt said. "You'll be letting everyone down. Plenty of other people work while they're having cancer treatment. Not sure why you think you're so precious."

I signed the leave forms and handed them over to my principal. "Before I change my mind," I said.

He didn't have to agree to it. It was personal leave – I was still getting paid. Replacing me would cost him extra money.

Guilt.

Except, he didn't replace me.

"See what you've done," Guilt said.

I had a four-day-a-week teaching load. I was responsible for half the ESL students. I'd effectively doubled my colleague's teaching load.

"Tut tut." Cancer shook her head. "All that work you've piled on to your teaching partner while you sit at home, reading your book and eating biscuits."

"That's not all I do," I replied, biscuit crumbs flying out of my mouth as I spat the words out.

But it was. And I knew it.

"I honestly don't mind," said my colleague. "I'll manage. You just focus on getting better." But I heard her words drag their feet. I heard her yawn.

"See!" said Cancer.

I ate another biscuit – a ginger nut, only fleetingly dunked in my coffee so it was able to be bitten but still had a nice crunch. These things take skill and practice. I chewed noisily, deliberately, with my mouth open. The crunch did well to drown out Cancer's contempt.

When you are the recipient of drawn-out medical interventions you surely, on occasion, have the right to hurl patience out the window of a fast-moving car in the middle lane of a highway to nowhere.

"I'm so sick of this!"

The home care nurse smiled her kind smile. "Just be patient," she said.

I was sick of being patient. Sick of being the patient. The bloody drain was still attached to my armpit four weeks after surgery. It was still draining, filling the bag with yuck a good week after the predicted removal date.

"Everybody is different," the nurse added.

Well, fuck that! I didn't want to be different. I was sick of being stuck to a stupid bag into which revolting slimy yellowish fluid dripped. The stupid thing leaked once. The smell was horrendous. I had to sleep on my back. I couldn't drive. Getting dressed to go out was an Olympic marathon event.

I was sick of it all. Sick of myself. Sick of relying on other people. Sick of having no hair. Sick of being sick.

"At least you're still alive," Guilt said.

"Well, I'm sick of that too," I snapped.

At that very moment, hearing those words, the whole world froze around me and held its collective breath. "What did you say?" it whispered. My friends, my colleagues, my family – I imagined them all turning to me, shock, horror, despair and their own guilt circling them like vultures.

"Well, I am," I said. "I'm sick of it all."

Guilt wrapped me in her suffocating embrace.

Guilt never left my side. She was there in my oncologist's waiting room, at the Zita Mary Clinic and in the Canberra Region Cancer Centre radiation clinic. She crept around, shadowing me with stealth and malintent. She hummed tunelessly in the back seat of the car as I drove to various appointments. She schlepped along after me as I walked up stairs and along corridors, skulked behind dusty plants or curled around the leg of the chair I sat upon as I pretended to read my book, painfully aware of all the other patients in various stages of ill-health.

There were all sorts.

The wrinkled and unsteady elderly, through to the young – too young. Overweight, underweight; the difference between a hessian sack filled to bursting with produce and one that's completely empty. Rosy-cheeked to cadaverous grey. Chrome-domed hairlessness to flowing locks that may or may not have been permanently attached – it's impossible to tell these days.

I watched them all over the rim of my glasses and from behind my book. Reading and re-reading the same paragraph umpteen times until my name was called, often well after my allotted time.

"Even the healthy-looking ones are sicker than you," Guilt whispered with its gym-sock breath.

Gym socks – the smell of lingering death. Stale. Overused. Forgotten.

Decay from the inside out. I'd noticed it in my own aura – my personal space – shortly after chemo had started. It was there all the time. No amount of soap or gel or floral spray could overcome it. I smelled it. I felt it. I tasted it.

It made me recoil from others. Others whose smells were stronger. Stronger than mine.

"See," said Guilt. "You're so lucky."

'You're so lucky'. A phrase echoed by others – friends, family, colleagues.

"Yes," I'd say, "I'm very lucky."

Luckier than those who had to have a second course of chemo because the first didn't quite work.

Luckier than those who had to have a mastectomy – or go back to get more chopped off because they 'hadn't quite got it all the first time'.

Luckier than those who'd recovered, then un-recovered, and were back to square one.

Luckier than those who weren't lucky at all – and could no longer be lucky.

Who the hell was I to feel distraught? Hard done by? Angry? Upset?

I was the lucky one.

"Right," said Cancer. Her voice was soft. Feeble. But still she spoke. "You keep thinking how lucky you are. It makes you complacent."

"Shut up," I said. But I didn't mean it. Sometimes Cancer's words were what I deserved – what I needed to hear.

The way guilt sounds

We left the doctor's office and walked outside. I turned to
my husband and said, "I'm sorry. I'm so sorry."
That's how I felt – so sorry for him that his wife had cancer.

~ Joan ~

I do remember thinking, though, that it was harder
for everyone else than it was for me.

~ Lyndall ~

After she left, I turned to my ex and said,
"How could I be so disconnected from this?
How could I be so not in the picture?"

~ Jenny ~

Everyone has their own experience that's unique to them and should be acknowledged for what it was. Although, sometimes it's hard not to feel guilty when I think about how lucky I was and then hear about what some other women are going through.

~ Janet ~

Some events in life play out on a roller-coaster, inducing sweaty-palmed anticipation of the inevitable ups and downs and fuelled by equal quantities of dread and delight.

Anticipation

n. looking forward to a future event or state, sometimes with an affective component (e.g. pleasure, anxiety).

I remember the first time I went on a roller-coaster. Not one of those namby-pamby roller-coasters that you don't need to wear a harness in because they barely move and don't go upside down.

No.

It was a real roller-coaster. One with two loops and a corkscrew. With a full-on, padded safety bar and a cushioned steel harness that squeezed the air right out of your lungs and left them like a deflated whoopee cushion.

I was twelve.

When it came to showground rides I was not a risk-taker. It wasn't about fear. I wasn't scared of heights or speed … or death, as it happens. The fear was a little more basic. It was a fear of losing my lunch, or whatever else I'd recently ingested, in front of and perhaps all over everybody.

You may laugh, but I've done it. From the top of a Ferris wheel, no less – the most insipid of showground rides.

On said day, after one revolution we were greeted back at the bottom of the wheel by a less-than-impressed operator who, when my friend asked if we could get off because I felt sick, said, "Yes. I wore it."

The Ferris wheel friend was not the same person as the roller-coaster friend. Although both were guilty of the same level of peer pressure. "Come on. You'll love it. It's not scary. It won't be any fun without you."

I tried to argue but couldn't come up with anything remotely convincing. I did not know this friend well enough to ask her if she minded wearing the chips with gravy I'd not long eaten, and if I had I suspect it would have made little difference.

We stood in the line.

It was long. It moved a shuffle-step a minute.

Then, without warning, we were at the front.

There was no escape. I was hemmed in – a gate on either side of me, and behind me two kids stood on tippy toes, both bright-eyed. They must have only just made the height minimum.

The whole time we'd been in the line, a narrative had been winding its way through my mind; a collection of short stories, if you like, each one detailing a potential case scenario of doom, destruction and … vomit.

A guy with cigarette breath and greasy hair strapped us in. He had a tattoo on his finger of a ring, with a skull where the stone should be. It's funny what details you remember. He gave the harness a jiggle. "Should be okay," he said.

Should?

"Should be?" I squeaked.

"Yeah, well … you know," he said. "It's old equipment." He laughed and winked as the carriage jolted forward.

If I was going to spew, maybe it would land on him.

We crawled slowly out of the tunnel. Whoever designed this particular roller-coaster was, I decided, a sadist. Who else would design a contraption such as this – one that jolted, squealed and rattled its way around a bend and towards a long, near vertical ascent, only to then tip people over the edge and send them into a vortex of bone-shaking spins and turns where your lips come close to flying off your face and your eyes dry out from the rush of wind.

And then it was over.

It was awesome.

I felt great.

My food was still intact in my stomach.

"Let's do it again!" I said to my friend, and we ran to join the queue which had since doubled in length.

Anyway, the point of that long-winded story is that first roller-coaster ride, for me, was the epitome of anticipation.

The epitome of that finger-tingling, smile-stretching, heart-racing excitement brought on by knowing there is something fun just around the corner.

The epitome of the gut-sinking, nail-chewing, heart-pounding doomsday fear brought on by knowing there is something life-destroying just around the corner.

Anticipation is the ultimate shapeshifter, moulding herself and fitting to suit every emotion from elation to trepidation.

Denial to Determination.

Hostility to Guilt.

It was my friend Anticipation who had me prepping weeks in advance for the school year I'd been so looking forward to.

It was Anticipation who had me avoiding making an appointment immediately upon discovery of 'the lump'.

And it was Anticipation who was by my side 24/7, fuelling my flames of frustration at my lack of fitness and general wellness after eight months of chemo, plus surgery and radiation.

Do you remember, as a kid, waiting 'forever' for some exciting event to occur – like Christmas or your birthday or a holiday – while you're just bursting with excitement? The days are agonisingly long. Everything moves at the slowest pace possible. Yet still that bubble of excitement keeps you happy and … well … excited.

My 'exciting event' was the end of treatment and the return to normality.

My world had slowed to a near standstill.

The difference between kids and adults is never more stark than when it comes to anticipation. While a kid's excitement bubble contains sweetness and fluffiness and sparkles, as an adult my excitement bubble was full of swearing, eye rolls and the need to punch something … hard.

It was the desperate need of Anticipation to burst this bubble that saw me knock back the 'extra week of radiotherapy' recommended by the radiologist I could not stand.

"You really shouldn't say that about a medical professional," Guilt said to me. "She's only doing her job. You aren't really in a position to judge her."

My dislike for this radiologist was something I refused to relinquish, despite Guilt's entreaties. "What medical professional repeatedly makes reference to the size of your breasts?" I argued back. Anger and Hostility rushed forward as I continued – it didn't take much to summon them right now. "For someone with breasts as large as yours …", "I'd expect more burning on people with such large breasts …" I mimicked her nasal voice inaccurately, but it made me feel good.

"The extra week of radiation will give you that extra level of protection," the radiologist said.

We were sitting in one of the consultation rooms in the Cancer Centre section of the hospital. Just me, her and a computer surrounded by yellowing walls, stale antiseptic and some seventies furniture. The lot of a public facility.

"How much extra protection?" I asked. As far as I was concerned, I was done. I'd had my eight weeks – that was what she'd told me initially – and now she was telling me to stay. That I wasn't done.

"About one per cent," she said. "It doesn't look like much but every bit counts, right?" She gave her squint-eyed smirk-smile that I suspected was supposed to be reassuring but really only had the effect of making me want to wipe it off with a steel scourer.

"One per cent of what?" I asked.

But she was moving on. "So – how are the burns?"

"They're fine," I said. "Minimal. Slightly uncomfortable, like an itchy rash." I gave her the teacher eye – a look well-honed by all teachers to stop students in their tracks without the need to utter a single word. It was a look that was meant to say, "Don't say it!"

She ignored it. "Really? You're very lucky, because women with breasts as large as yours usually suffer terribly from burns." She looked me up and down, then pointedly stared at my chest. "Are you sure?"

There was that smile again.

My jaw clenched.

Every. Bloody. Time.

Six times, I'd seen her. Each time, she'd felt the need to comment on the size of my breasts.

"Jealousy," I'd ranted to a friend the third time the radiologist had said it. "Just because her chest could moonlight as an ironing board."

"That's sort of inappropriate," my friend said. "No male could get away with saying that."

For a moment I wondered if she was referring to me and my ironing board comment.

"I should report her," I said, my tone full of self-righteous disgust, both towards the so-called medical professional and the fact that I knew full well I wouldn't make any such report.

And I hadn't. Yet here she was again, going for the hexad.

"You know to ask the nurses for gels and bandages. The burns will come. Women like you …"

I cut her off. "Yes. I know." The teacher voice. "Back to that one per cent you mentioned …"

"What?" she frowned.

Her state of confusion was deeply satisfying and I bathed in it while she contorted her face in an attempt to regain control over the appointment. Then she spoke and ruined the moment.

"Oh, yes. It decreases your chance of recurrence a bit more. You responded well to chemotherapy and …" She continued to throw facts and figures at me. Pointed out the inherent dangers associated with lymph node clearances.

When she finally stopped to draw breath, I jumped in. "What I'm hearing is that an extra couple of weeks—"

"Nine days," she interrupted.

"An extra couple of weeks of coming in here every weekday for several hours and getting fried, not to mention the half-hour trip each way and the half hour it takes to find a park, plus the very likely chance a machine will be broken so my frying will be delayed by what could be several more hours … all of that will only reduce my chances of more cancer by the tiniest amount. A single per cent?"

It may seem that I resented the care I'd been given at this facility. I didn't. The staff at the radiation department were truly wonderful. They'd sit and chat. They always smiled and said hello, but didn't expect you to engage in conversation if you didn't want to. There was a lady who gave out donuts, offered with instant coffee or tea as she pushed around a trolley with a wonky wheel. "I'm sorry about the coffee," she'd say, "but the donuts are the nicest around. Pink icing." But, in all honesty, I was so done. I didn't want to be here anymore. Plus, it was a pain in the arse trying to get a park every day.

"A single per cent," I repeated, to be clear. "Just one?"

"Just under a per cent, actually." She shifted in her chair. Tried to stare me down. Turned back to her computer after I won the staring contest. "Well, most patients would take this opportunity to do whatever they can to minimise the risks."

Suddenly, I had this image of her as one of those Muppet characters – it didn't really matter which one – flouncing off the stage with a flick of the head and a high-pitched "harumph!"

I zipped up my bag, finding the sharpness and finality of the 'ZIP!' to be somewhat satisfying.

There was an ensuing argument, albeit a brief one.

Her face screamed her desire to tell me how stupid I was being, and I willed her to voice it so I could retaliate and share my thoughts about her.

She didn't.

Smart move.

I sat, knees together, handbag on my lap. I was poised to stand and leave but, like a good girl, waiting for her permission.

"Okay." She sighed. Deliberate. "That's your decision. Which means this will be your last appointment with me, unless you decide to continue your six-monthly reviews with me rather than your surgeon?" It was framed as a question.

As if!

I nodded. "Thank you," I said as I stepped out in the corridor.

"Good luck." Her words echoed behind me. An afterthought, perhaps – although, if I were her, I'd have been just as glad to be rid of me as I was to be done with her.

At reception, a lovely man with a coffee stain on his shirt asked if I needed to make my review appointment.

"No, I'm all good." I walked away with undisguised haste, in a hurry to get home where I could remove my bra. Agony – it was rubbing like sandpaper against my radiation burns.

I argued with myself over my decision as I drove home. Was I being an idiot? Had I let my intense dislike of a medical professional cloud my judgement?

"Why did you do it?" Cancer asked. Her voice was an autumn leaf, dry and brittle, flaking around the edges and crumbling away to dust. "You had the chance to close the door in my face. And you didn't."

"One per cent," I said. "The door is never fully closed."

"But still," Cancer went on, "the door is open just that one per cent wider now."

"Whatever," I said.

In my mind, I was done. I'd done my time and was ready to move on. Ready to get my life back. I had things to do.

"You do, indeed," Anticipation jumped in – the voice of a sea breeze at dusk. "You can get back to the gym. Back to dragon boating. You're on the team to paddle in Florence; how cool is that! A trip to Italy."

Like a child who'd been dosed up with red cordial and chocolate cake Anticipation prattled on, reminding me of all the things I'd put on hold and all the things I'd dreamed of and planned for 'when I was better'.

I had my life back!

The newly-realised freedom of not having my weekday plans dictated by the timing of radiology appointments. The gradual clawing back of my energy. The sprouting of hair once again atop my head.

"I hope it doesn't stay this curly," I said to my hairdresser as I eyed the steel-wool grey pubes that had sprung from my scalp.

"It should straighten again," my hairdresser said. "I've heard it does."

"Maybe it won't be so thick this time round," I said.

And we laughed and laughed as he ran his fingers through my curls. "I'm not so sure about that," he smiled wickedly. "It might be even thicker." He laughed again at my expression in the mirror. "It should be long enough for colour. If you have time, I can do it now."

Two hours later, I walked out of his salon headwear-free for the first time in over eight months. The breeze was cold, pricking its way through to my scalp, but I was buggered if I was going to cover it up.

Never again will I underestimate the power of your hair for making you feel whole and human.

"Are you looking forward to going back to school?" my hairdresser had asked as I paid.

I'd been asked that question multiple times. "Yes, of course," I'd answered.

Each time, I'd forced cheer into my response while Anticipation made a feeble attempt at a happy dance.

In truth, though, I really did not want to go back to school. I'd had three terms to think about my life. My career. My future. Three terms to reflect on how much I'd been looking forward to the start of the year – and why. Three terms to realise it had been a front; a way of protecting myself from the misery of feeling stuck.

"You should go easy," my doctor said. "Don't overdo it or you could set your recovery back."

A spark of hope ignited.

My oncologist concurred. "You'll still be feeling the effects of all those drugs for some time. Go slowly."

Anticipation glowed then shadowed – a show of solidarity, perhaps? An attempt to get me to take things one step at a time. Or perhaps a sign of my conflicting emotions.

Both medical professionals agreed I should take Term 4 off as well. Take the time to properly recover from what was essentially eight months of trauma.

"Not a bad idea," said Anticipation. "You are aware I never stated exactly what we were looking forward to? Besides, is it not a woman's prerogative to change her mind?"

Four months later, I was back at school. Still not keen, but feeling much more spritely and full of determined hope to make some sort of change.

Anticipation's shapeshifting tendencies revealed themselves on the eve of my yearly mammogram. My first regular one since diagnosis.

I had felt Cancer shift when I made the appointment, though she stayed mercifully silent.

Anticipation, on the other hand, did not possess the same control.

"What if …" she said. She struggled to form the words, her face ashen. She sent goosebumps prickling along my arms.

I breathed deeply as I waited to be called in. I stared at the others in the waiting room of the imaging centre. I wondered why they were there.

My own smile was wooden as I was collected and invited to gown up … and then ungown to have my breasts squeezed, one at a time, smushed between metal and plastic.

"I won't be long," the technician said as she took the slides to the radiologist on duty.

I sat in the tall-backed chair, holding the gown closed. My heart raced as Anticipation stood by my side. Her cold, grey hand on my chest, she whispered what-ifs into my ear and I thought stupid thoughts to drown her out.

An eternity passed.

The door opened to the beeps and light chatter of the corridor. "You're all good," I was told.

I left, weaving my way through the maze of corridors, through reception and out into the hot February sun. Anticipation skipped by my side like an excited child.

"One down," said Cancer.

The rest of my life, stretched out in front of me, darkened momentarily at her truth. She was right. One down. How many to go?

Anticipation stepped up and slapped Cancer away. "Seize the day!" she cried.

She ran ahead, bouncing and singing. At the road she stopped. Her head dropped. Her back slumped. She turned back, reached for Cancer and hugged her tight in a display of remorse and solidarity.

Denial followed, dragging Shock in her wake, as Determination clap-clapped behind them like an impatient schoolteacher. Anger and Hostility loitered even further back, wanting to be seen but not directly associated with us. Guilt crept, as usual, around the edges. She was like a stalker, biding her time and waiting for her opportunity to pounce.

Cancer's voice floated back on the breeze. "You'll never be free of us," she said. Then she called to a shadow over to our left, "Oh hey, I was wondering when you'd show up. You've taken your time."

The way anticipation sounds

My hair had started growing back – it was all of about three millimetres – and I was sick of wearing the turban. "The turban's coming off," I announced at work. "I hope nobody minds but I'm done with all of that. Here I am." Of course, they were all good about it.

~ April ~

"I'm here," I said. "Let's just do it. Now."
I didn't want to muck around.

They'd already brought the trolley in, so they were going to do it anyway. It wasn't really a choice. Afterwards, it was the waiting – waiting for the results. All I was thinking that whole time was, oh man. What now?'

~ Janet ~

I don't want to die. I don't want to leave my children.
I want a wonderful life. I deserve a wonderful life.

~ Natalie ~

Afterwards, I threw all my paperwork down in a box in the garage. I didn't need to look at it. I didn't need it in the house. A couple of my friends who've had breast cancer too went and found the paperwork. They started going through it and I just said, "I'll go and get the shredder and shred it right now." I didn't want it around and I didn't want to start wondering whether I should have had this or had that.

~ Denise ~

Delicious trepidation is a far cry from gut-wrenching paralysis, yet fear treads boldly in all domains and is always in control, despite me telling myself otherwise.

Fear

***n.** a basic, intense emotion aroused by the detection of imminent threat, involving an immediate alarm reaction that mobilizes the organism by triggering a set of physiological changes.*

Does anyone else delight in the adrenaline rush produced by fear?

Perhaps you love-hate going into those haunted houses in sideshow alley? Or maybe you love-hate watching horror movies late at night during a storm? Whatever it is, you crave that stereotypical thumping heart that echoes through your chest cavity and into your ears. You indulge in holding your breath until your chest tightens to the point of pain and threatens to expel itself in a gasping gush, thus revealing your presence within your ineffective hiding place. Your hand tingles at the thought of the white-knuckled grip on the nearest object, the tight jaw and slow grind of teeth as your inner child whimpers and cries, "Oh shit, oh shit …"

I am one of those people. I like to scare myself.

Horror is my genre of choice. Not the blood and guts, bring up your lunch style of horror – that's not true horror. Mind you, I have watched my fair share of slasher horror, mainly during my teenage slumber party years. *Blood Beach*, anyone? OMG!

What I like is the type of horror that leaves crescent indents on the heel of my hand, causes shallow, barely-there breaths and surreptitious side-glances, and necessitates the construction of a protective cushion tower around which I watch the screen through splayed fingers.

As if a tower of cushions and a bony hand could protect me should the yellow-eyed demon spring from the television to suck out my soul and enter its vessel through my silent-screaming mouth, leaving only a whiff of a black sulphur-smoked trail.

But it's better than nothing.

I must really love that sense of fear because I watch such things late at night when the house creaks and shifts. Night houses breathe life into their invisible inhabitants, who then walk the hallway, tip-tapping on doors and scraping nails down walls. Who follow me to bed where I lay, eyes wide and dry, staring into the pitch-black, knowing that, when I do sleep, they will enter my mind and toy with my dreams until the line between unconsciousness and reality is blurred. At this point, I don't know if the presence that chased me through the dampened undergrowth, caught me at the door and held me down so I was unable to draw breath was real or a figment of my overactive, horror-movie-saturated mind.

I used to sleepwalk as a child. This curse lasted right through to my early adolescence, when my somnambulism rose to its ultimate crest and saw me jolted awake in the middle of the bush, far above the campsite where my Year 7 cohort feigned sleep and the teachers played cards with bleary eyes, waiting until the giggles and whispers ceased so they too could go to bed. They didn't catch me, the teachers, though not for want of trying. I listened to the PE teacher's feet pound behind me as I wrenched open the door of my cabin and threw myself into my sleeping bag, squeezing my eyes shut against the torchlight that searched every bunk in the room.

That night, I worked out a way to stop the sleepwalking. But I still don't have a way to stop the fear of it happening again.

So, yes, I love the rush of fear … when I am in control of it.

Of course, it doesn't always wait for an invitation.

"You must be pleased that it's all over," a colleague said.

We were sitting in the school staffroom, just the two of us. The lingering spice of someone's curry mingled with the ever-present microwave popcorn aroma, creating a slightly stomach-turning fug throughout the small room. I don't know why school staffrooms always smell of popcorn. Perhaps it's one of those unsolved staffroom mysteries, like the absence of forks, or lumpy milk.

I'd been back at school after my 'year off' for less than a week and I was already plagued by the bite of bitterness.

"Yes," I said out loud, in response to my colleague's non-question.

Inside, however, my sarcastic voice took a bit of an adolescent, 'are you serious?' tone. All over, I thought. Over? Okay, so chemo was over. Surgery was over. Radiation was over. But it wasn't over.

"Damn straight," Cancer croaked. "And don't refer to me as 'it'. That's rude."

Cancer was a mere shell of her former self. A wisp of a memory. The tail of a nightmare with no substance.

My colleague prattled on, "… and you can get back to normal now …"

"Absolutely. It's so good," I mused out loud. "I'm so pleased. It's. All. Over. Yes. Back to normal."

Normal, I thought. What's normal?

"Although," I added, eyeballing my colleague, "normal is relative."

"I … I … didn't mean …"

"Of course you didn't," I said. Thankfully the bell rang, putting her out of her misery.

"You've made me intolerant," I said to Cancer.

"I've done nothing of the sort," Cancer retorted. "You've always been intolerant. I just set it free to help you not give a flying fuck."

She was right.

It was liberating.

I should thank her for it.

Normality is definitely relative though, I thought as I let the class that wasn't my own through the door.

My normal now was three-weekly treks to the Zita Mary Clinic to get

Herceptin pumped into my thigh. Did they do the right side last time, or the left?

Normal is nightly medication for the foreseeable future.

Normal is regular bone scans, mammograms, ultrasounds. Waiting for results. Twice-yearly visits to specialists where I strip from the waist up and lay, staring at the white ceiling, while they push and knead my chest.

"Breathe in," they say. "Breathe out. Any pain? Any discomfort?"

Always no.

So far.

Each day as it comes.

And normal is the stone in my gut every time I feel a niggle, a spasm, a twinge. It's the stone that weighs me down and pulls me under. It's looking Fear in the eye before kicking away and breaking back to the surface with sharp, rasping gasps.

I should say here, this Fear was not the same fear I coveted and sought while watching movies and reading Stephen King. Rather than wrapping my body in a cloak of tingles, this Fear frequently covered me in a weighted shroud. It would pull me down into the dark depths of semi-consciousness where there was nobody but me and I could invite nobody in.

In the privacy of my own space, this Fear reigns supreme. For this fear is mine, and is not to be disseminated through my family or placed onto my close friends.

"We'll do some tests," my doctor says, ever vigilant each time I see her to describe the niggles and twinges. "Eliminate the nasties."

I've never been a hypochondriac. Five years on, is that what I am now? The thought filters through my mind, teasing and tickling at the edges.

Maybe it's nothing, I think. Every time.

It's probably nothing.

But what if it's something?

That 'oh, it's nothing' nearly landed me in hot water five years ago, I remind myself. Denial struggles with me every … single … time, as she did back then. But now I am stronger and while I may wait, delaying the call for a day or two, I eventually make it.

"Can I make an appointment with Tina?" I ask.

"Oh, she's booked out for the next couple of weeks," the receptionist inevitably responds. "I can get you in to see Dr So-and-so …"

My doctor is always booked out. You need to have a crystal ball to anticipate ailments a good three months in advance. "It's regarding the breast cancer," I always say.

Somehow, an appointment is always found.

This Fear is not the fear I choose.

It's not the fear that gives me a lift and makes my blood rush and my skin tingle.

This Fear is my new cancer. Not actual cancer, but cancer-like in its stealth and destruction.

Mid-2022, as I was approaching my magic 'five years since diagnosis' mark, I started to experience no end of niggles, electric tingles, aches and weird sensations. They'd come. They'd go. Some stayed for longer than others. All stayed for long enough to plant their seeds of doubt. Long enough to be watered and tended by Fear.

"I know it's in my head," I said to my doctor. "At least, I hope it's in my head; my mind. Overreacting. Anxious. More anxious than it needs to be." I gibbered, nonsensical even to my own ears.

Five vials of blood was what it took. My eyes widened at the sight. I was impressed the nurse had managed to find a vein the first time – that's skill. But I honestly thought she was going to suck me dry.

Umpteen blood tests all came back showing … nothing. Nothing at all. Nothing out of the ordinary. The bone scan and ultrasound both agreed.

"I'm coming up to five years," I said to my doctor.

"Why is five years so important?" she asked.

"I don't know. It's just the number everyone talks about."

I looked it up on the Cancer Council website when I got home: *Cancer is most likely to recur in the first five years after treatment ends.*

That's why. It had been five years since I was diagnosed.

Then it hit me.

I still had eight months to go until I met the 'five years after treatment ends' milestone. The scar under my armpit seized up as it does intermittently. Did it last for longer this time?

What happens after that five-year mark? Cancer magically disappears?

A smooth little niche had already been carved out by my Fear. An escape tunnel between my mind and my gut. She'd been gently carving it away over the last five years, like salty ocean spray and the ebb and flow of the tide smoothing rocks and sculpting caves. Imperceptible to the naked eye, but obvious over a span of time.

She'd lain in wait, biding her time. Not once did she reveal herself during my actual treatment. Fear wasn't there for my diagnosis, my chemo, my surgery or my radiation. Denial may have had a hand in this, weaving her anaesthetic to ensure Fear stayed undetected. Or perhaps it was a case of trust in the medical profession? The strength of my grandmother? The swear book? The words of a dear friend who has been and is still going through so much. "Carpe diem," she says all the time. "Seize the day."

Who knows what it was, but I wanted to know why Fear had decided to make her presence known now.

"You changed me," I accused Fear.

Fear cowered. Arm in arm with Cancer, they propped each other up.

"You snuck up on me," I said. "You've made me paranoid."

Fear blinked at me. Gave a slight tilt of the head. Affirmation.

"She only does what you allow her to do," said Cancer.

I hated it when Cancer was right.

"So, I've won." Cancer said.

Is this all there is? A life of doom and gloom. Of the spectre of Cancer hanging over my head? Of letting Fear rule. Of letting Cancer get away with it all, giving her the satisfaction of a victory over my mind, if not my body.

"No," I said.

Did I mean it?

Say it like you mean it!

"Hell-fucking-no."

Fear stared at me with red-lined eyes and shrunk back into the deep.

I revelled in my small victory.

My dad's voice came from above. "That's my girl," he said, strong and clear. I wished I could hug him.

Next to him, I pictured my grandmother. She'd been gone for over four years by now, and I'd missed her every single day. She smiled and nodded. My grandfather took her hand and winked at me. His cheeky-boy grin spoke volumes. "Never give in," he said.

Cancer sat back. "Fine," she said. "Whatever."

The way fear sounds

The fear is real. It's always with me. Every now and then, my mind switches over and I start with the 'should haves'.

~ Clare ~

My first chemo session was terrifying.

We went in and they got me all set up and explained what was going to happen. They also explained things like how after chemo it was important to flush the toilet twice and things like that. Then a lady approached me – and I nearly fainted in fright. She was wearing a big purple outfit, with big purple gloves and was holding a purple bucket.
I just found it all so scary.

~ Marion ~

Oddly enough, I've found I'm no longer scared of the breast cancer itself. I am, however, scared about not knowing either way.

~ Jenny ~

I didn't know. I was panicking. I wasn't sleeping.
I wasn't eating. It's what stress does to me.
I was worried about my job. And my son.

What about my son?

~ Che ~

Watching your mum, or anyone you love, going through
all of this – it's like being on your own emotional roller-
coaster, but different to the one Mum was on. It was scary.
For me, at first, it was a bit like: is this really happening?
It is really cancer? I was pretty much thinking like that
until she actually went in to have surgery.

~ Nadine ~

Salt-water gratitude flowed, healing me as I reflected upon my year. It sheared away the ties that had so long bound me to my past life and carved a path for me to embrace the opportunity to start again.

Gratitude

__n.__ a sense of thankfulness and happiness in response to receiving a gift, either a tangible benefit (e.g. a present, favor) given by someone or a fortunate happenstance (e.g. a beautiful day).

Perhaps you're surprised to see a chapter about gratitude in a book about a breast cancer blip? Then again, maybe you're not. After all, surely people who've had breast cancer and 'survived' would be full of gratitude for many things, from the medical team to family and friends. Gratitude is, after all, very important for healing. To offer thanks. To stop wallowing in self-pity and 'woe is me'.

At some point, we all have to move on. When we are ready. When Gratitude has done her rounds.

Apart from my medical team, the people in my life that Gratitude had the most time for were those who accepted the way I needed to deal with what was happening in my life.

My personal trainer, Bryan, offered the best example of recognising what I needed. He let me slide away when I 'just couldn't face it' but kept me positive throughout and got me straight back on track when I was ready. "Muscle memory," he said when I lamented how much strength I'd lost over an eight-month period. "It'll come back quick and you'll be stronger before you know it." He was right.

Everyone needs someone like that in their corner.

My good friends. My writing buddies. My family. My colleagues. My dragon boating team. So many people who rallied around but gave me my space.

"Some didn't, though," I said.

"So what," Gratitude said. "The people who really matter did."

Of course, she was right.

The gruff people were the ones that I remember the most, and the ones that Gratitude hung around with the most.

"That dragon boat woman," Gratitude reminds me, "the one who took your daughter to and from training and told you that you looked funny when your hair started growing back. The one who got you back out on the water with the 'pink ladies' on Wednesdays at lunch time once your radiation burns had healed. She's a good egg." Gratitude snorted. "Gruff, but a good one."

Again, she was right.

'That dragon boat woman' was also the one who got me on the dragon boat to paddle in Florence.

"I've only just had leave," I protested when she told me the dates.

"Pah. And?" she said. "As if that was leave. Are you coming or what?"

Guilt spoke to me briefly about taking more time off so soon after I'd had a whole year away from work, but with the help of my principal and that dragon boat woman I managed to get her to shut up fairly quickly.

"Don't be ridiculous," my principal said when I voiced Guilt's words. "Last year was hardly a holiday, now, was it?"

I filled in the leave form. He signed it.

"I'm in," I said to that dragon boat woman.

"Good," that dragon boat woman said. "You all deserve it. Now get to training."

And so it was that less than a year after I got the 'all clear', and only six months after I'd returned to school from my year of 'leave', I was on a plane with my husband and kids, heading for Italy.

"Told you she was a good egg," said Gratitude, all smugness and knowing. I was willing to give her that.

We'd all been through the ups and downs of the previous year. We'd all come out the other end. Unscathed but changed. We all deserved a celebration.

"Might as well make the most of it," my husband said after we'd decided to take our time and spend a little over a month in Italy. Some of that time was during our school holidays, but most of it wasn't. The kids would catch up. My class would survive. Nobody is indispensable.

The day we were booked to fly out was actually my birthday. But that was fine. We wanted to fly to Singapore first and the only direct flight left Canberra at 11 pm. I had the whole day.

I spent several hours with my grandmother on my birthday. Sitting on the side of a bed in a hospital ward wasn't the ideal way to celebrate one's arrival into the world, but it was what it was and I was grateful to have her to myself.

Nanna was in good spirits – outwardly at least. On close examination, though, her face was weary, more so than when I'd seen her a few days before. Still, we laughed over something silly we overheard her roommate say as we shared a large square of mud cake in celebration of the start of my forty-ninth year. We talked. We sat, companionably silent.

We tried not to think of the future.

I wasn't overly successful there; a failure not helped by my recollection of what some bright spark with an atrocious sense of humour (read that as 'arsehole', if you like) had scribbled on Nanna's in-patient whiteboard a few weeks ago.

Angel airways. Feathery letters written quickly in the 'Discharge Plan' box.

I only needed to read it once to know what it implied.

Anger, who I hadn't had to deal with for a while, had reared up out of nowhere – zero to a hundred. I'd scrubbed off the words, thankful for once that my grandmother couldn't see that far. If the person who'd written those words had revealed themselves to me I can only guess at what I would've done.

"Can you raise the head of the bed a bit?" Nanna asked, pulling me out of my memory funk for a moment. "My bum hurts."

Nobody should have to spend weeks in an uncomfortable hospital bed, eating sub-standard slop and being patronised by some staff members who clearly thought that old and immobile also meant stupid and hearing-impaired. Thank goodness these attitudes were few and far between, but sadly they are the ones you often recall first.

Too soon, it was time to go. Our house-sitter was coming by to drop her gear off and I needed to be there to let her in. Hand her the keys. Mundane stuff that had to be done.

Goodbyes are not my strong point. Should I consider myself lucky that I knew this goodbye would truly be the last one? That it would be the last time I'd be sharing morning tea with her; the last time I'd see her?

Here's a fact straight from the heart – last goodbyes suck even more when you know for a fact they are the last.

Walking away from her, down the sterile corridor and out to my car, I was both numb and robotic. It took every ounce of strength not to turn back.

I wish I hadn't had to say goodbye. Not then. Not ever.

Yet, I was grateful for the time we had. So many years. It had never failed to astound me how many of my peers had grown up without knowing their grandparents. I had all four of my grandparents until I was in my twenties and my Nanna and Pop, on Mum's side, for over forty-five years.

You have to be grateful for that.

I was also grateful that Nanna had been around during this period of my life. I hated that she blamed herself and felt guilty even though it wasn't her doing, but being able to share the little things and just spend time with her was invaluable.

Five years down the track and Gratitude still sits with me. She's there for every mammogram and ultrasound, holding my hand tight until I find out that I'm good for another year. She's there cheering my kids on as they achieve milestones and reminding me that, although they are bloody hard work at times, I'm thankful that I'm here to be part of it all. And when I start to doubt the intentions of people around me, Gratitude clears her throat as a reminder that I'm surrounded by good people.

But, above all else, Gratitude reserves most of her energy for Cancer.

It's the truth.

I was shocked when that thought first popped into my brain. Who in their right mind would be grateful for having been hit by Cancer?

Me, as it turns out.

In fact, Gratitude shapes my stock-standard response when anybody suggests I must have had an awful year in 2017.

"Oh, you poor thing," they say when they find out about the breast cancer. "That must have been terrible for you. What a horrible year you must have had."

"Actually," I say, "yeah, the chemo wasn't nice and the surgery sucked. Didn't much like radiation or my radiologist either. However, treatment aside, it was the best year of my life."

Most of the time the only response is a slack jaw. Or a laugh. Or "For real?"

"Yep," I say. Then I change the subject, leaving them to ponder and think their own thoughts because, in all honesty, I'm quite comfortable with that answer.

My attitude and response to 'poor you' has floored many a person in the last five years. I may have lost 'friends' and respect. However, I will continue to believe it and share it because I stand by it.

For me!

I have to emphasise the 'for me' bit because I know full well that I run the risk of being howled down as dismissive of the much more tumultuous journeys others have had, and continue to have. Not only the people for whom cancer came calling, but for their family and friends, especially those who may have been left behind.

But, say it I have. And I continue to say it.

"You surely don't mean that?"

"Yes," I say. "Yes, I do."

"You're taking the piss."

"No, you're wrong. It would have been horrible."

"You don't need to be so brave."

All of the above – and more – has been said to me, but I do actually mean it.

"I don't want to be disrespectful," I remember saying at some point, "but surely my experience and my feelings on the whole year are just as valid as the next person's?"

"You are bloody disrespectful," Guilt spoke up in a 'hands on hips and feet firmly-planted' sort of voice. "You should be thankful you survived, not cheering because cancer fixed your life."

And I am. Thankful. Grateful. For many things.

Without Cancer I wouldn't have been able to join Dragons Abreast Canberra. It's a pretty drastic way to join a dragon boating team. We have pretty stringent admission criteria; almost akin to being a sacrificial lamb. Admittedly, I wavered for a couple of years. My original team had given me so much so I stayed as a dual member for a while, but things change. People move on. And eventually I moved over solely to DAC because that was what was right for me, and still is.

It's all about me and what I need. Nobody else. For the record, I'm bloody grateful for that attitude shift as well. Selfish. Self-indulgent. Whatever it is, I am happier being my own person.

Gratitude and I have now come to a complete understanding.

But it's with hindsight that I developed this attitude. Before Cancer came to stay, my life was like pedalling a stationary bike – lots of work to get nowhere. Tedious. Feeling stuck but not knowing what else to do.

Cancer gave me the opportunity to get off that bike. Cancer made me reflect on all the things I was doing despite not wanting to do them. Cancer and Fear and Guilt and Anticipation and Determination and Hostility and Denial and Anger and Shock – they all banded together to kick me in the butt and yell and scream and plead with me to re-evaluate who I was, effect my own change and start living my life the way I wanted. Otherwise, what was the point of going through all the chemo, the nausea, the hair loss, the burns and the surgery?

There was no point.

Cancer made me realise I wasn't happy with who I was.

And if I wasn't happy with myself, how could I make other people happy and do the right thing by them while still staying true to myself?

"So you finally realised?" Cancer asked.

"Realised what?" I said.

"You needed me."

"I used you." I shrugged. I shut the lid on her box and stowed her away in the cobwebby depths of my mind, behind the things that matter.

The way gratitude sounds

I did the jet boat thing over the rapids.
We went on a helicopter ride. I did paragliding.

I'm going to do all of this, I thought.

~ Elly ~

I was so happy when I finished. I bought chocolates for
the technicians. I bought chocolates for the people at the
reception desk. Actually, when I finished chemo,
I baked a big cake for the staff. I kept saying to people,
"Don't take this the wrong way but
I hope I never see you again."

~ Deb ~

It's beautiful in the way that it does open up other experiences and other relationships. You come to see things differently; not through rose-coloured glasses, but things take on a different meaning. That's beautiful. For example, you see a sunset and realise they are so much better than they were pre-cancer. You stop sweating over the big things – and the little things – because what's the point?

Having cancer puts things back into perspective.

~ Kathy ~

Not everyone was an arsehole, though.

~ Natalie ~

Paddling for Vi

My grandmother passed away while we were in Italy. She'd hung on for six days after I spoke to her for the last time. The phone call came from my mother, not long after we'd returned to our little apartment in the beautiful hill-town of Vico Equense having spent a glorious day swimming and feasting in Sorrento for my daughter's birthday.

"She's gone," was all she said. Or all I heard, at any rate.

I was numb but I couldn't cry. I'd done all my crying on the day I'd walked out of her hospital room and the first day of the regatta when I last spoke with her.

We also had a little over a week remaining of our time in Italy.

"Don't come home." Nanna's words echoed in my mind. "You enjoy your holiday."

We did, although it had lost a tiny bit of its sparkle.

Her funeral was on July 24. I sat with Mum when we got back while she organised yet another service – first Dad's, then Pop's and now Nanna's. I wrote a remembrance piece as I'd done for Dad and Pop, but this time I knew I wouldn't be able to read it.

In Florence, at the end of the regatta, all participants were given a medal. They'd gone all out – a heavy, crystal-like disc the size of my palm, which hung on a smooth pink lanyard and came in a pale-pink velvet pouch.

At the end of the funeral, I took that medal out of the pouch and placed it over Nanna's coffin.

"We paddled for you, Nanna," I whispered.

A couple of days later I was back at training. It was sunny and relatively warm for July, and I'd arrived early – mainly to get a park.

'That dragon boat woman' was there. She was always early, arriving well ahead of time to uncover and set up the boat. I went down to give her a hand.

She finished tying on the safety bag and looked up at me. "You put your Florence medal on your grandmother's coffin," she said. It sounded accusatory but I knew it wasn't. That was her way.

"Yes," I said.

"Thought so." She reached into her pocket. Pulled out a pale-pink velvet pouch. "Here. I picked up a spare."

I took the pouch from her hand. "Thank you," I said. I very much doubted there were spares as every cent was accounted for in Florence.

"We may have paddled for Vi," she said, "but your grandmother would have been proud of you, and she'd want you to have that medal."

I've never really been one for crying in public. That was how I knew the news was bad.

I do not wish to experience that sense of not being in control ever again. And I won't.

I simply won't allow it.

And in the end …

Tears. Loss. That was then. At the beginning. Five years ago. When I thought my life would end. But it didn't. And sometimes I wonder why. Why was I the lucky one? How?

Of course it was bad. The whole year was bad. Cancer is bad.

You'll be used to Cancer having a voice by now. And if I were to succumb to her demands and give her the chance for one last say, she'd start by boring her spindly fingers into the scar that marks the place where my lymph nodes once sat. She'd be twisting the scar tissue inwards, pulling it into a searing cramp to emphasise her words. "Of course I'm bad," she would say. "I instil great fear into humans. I instilled great fear into you. I made you sick. I continue to make you scared. I will always be in control."

Cancer is both physically controlled in my body and out of control in my mind.

Does that mean she's in control?

"Of course it does," Cancer snapped.

At that moment, I knew.

I knew I had to take back the control. Take back the control the only way I really knew how – by writing about it.

And so, you've just read the cancer story I swore I was never going to write. Although, I'm quite sure it's not the cancer story people would have expected.

It's the cancer story that has laid bare all my emotions, my innermost thoughts and my fears. The ones I have never shared with anyone – not even my closest friends or family.

Will they be surprised?

Probably. Or maybe not. It depends how well they truly know me.

"Do you even know yourself?" If there's one thing Cancer does, it speaks the truth when nobody wants to hear it.

If I were to put my pre-cancer self and my post-cancer self side-by-side, we'd physically look the same. But if I peeled away the physical layers, revealing my inner selves, there would be little to call similar.

You may have resonated with some of the things I've said in these chapters. Cried at some. Disagreed with some. But the point is that by writing this story I took the control back from Cancer. I named her and all her emotional minions for what they are.

In so many ways, 2017 was indeed a horrible year. I wouldn't wish the experience on anyone. But, if I could turn back time, I wouldn't change a thing.

I would not change the time I spent with Cancer.

Cancer altered me. Sure, that could be construed as Cancer having control, but I refuse to think of it that way.

Before I walked, huffing and red-faced, with Cancer, I was unable to accept – let alone reveal – my true self. I was a very private person. Constrained by what people thought about me. Always wanting to do the 'right' thing, lest I be laughed at or thought less of. Pleasing others even if it meant being uncomfortable and unhappy and, sometimes, full of self-hate.

The whole shift I experienced during and after my cancer treatment is not unlike the theory I have about dementia. Like what happened with my grandmother, Edna. Once dementia starts taking hold and you lose your inhibitions and your sense of social correctness, your true self is free to come out and slap everyone in the face.

I feel that Cancer had the same effect on me. She allowed my true self to emerge.

The true self that doesn't say yes to things she doesn't want to do.

The true self that calls bullshit when she sees it and says what she thinks rather than what she knows people want to hear.

The true self that puts herself first – for the first time in her life.

That's the person I am now, but it is most definitely not the person I was before. The person I was before would never have made the statement I am about to make here.

> *Cancer afforded me the ability to unlock my true self and forced me to 'live'.*

After forty-seven years on this earth, my year in Cancer's company was my turning point.

I would not go back.

Final musings from a dragon boat

I plan on having a lot more chapters in my book.

~ Clare ~

There are positives to cancer: realising how wonderful my husband is; becoming part of the dragon boating community; having curls for the first time ever when my hair grew back.

~ Joan ~

It would have been good to have other supporters to talk to. Sort of like unleashing your burden onto someone else but not the person who actually has the cancer. Helping someone out through their cancer treatment is such a huge thing and while there's lots of support for those people, there doesn't seem to be a lot for the supporters.

~ Nadine ~

I guess, right from when I was diagnosed and knew what my treatment path would consist of, I viewed all of this as a journey – or a detour, if you like. One where I'd veer off on another pathway for a bit but then just come back onto my usual track. It was never going to be the case. You never really get back on the exact same track that you left.

~ Lyndall ~

Occasionally, I find myself thinking, 'Surely I didn't actually have cancer?' Cancer is something that happens to other people.

~ Denise ~

Why don't we talk about this? The end of treatment is certainly not the end of it at all.

~ Gillian ~

Appreciation

Writing a book is, I believe, best done in isolation. The opinions of many, or even one, can cloud your way and lead to self-doubt and second guessing. Worst-case scenario is that the book never sees the light of day in a published form.

However, producing a book – to use a clichéd term – takes a village. From those who encouraged and enthused and asked "Are you finished yet? I can't wait to read it," through to the people at the coalface, the graphic designer, photographer and typesetter, there are so many people I want to acknowledge and thank. I am petrified I will miss some of you and I apologise in advance if I do miss you; please know that I appreciate you and Guilt will ensure I don't forget my error.

So, to the expressions of appreciation, in no particular order.

All of the ladies in Dragons Abreast Canberra (DAC) dragon boating team. Thank you for being you. I learn from you every day and being part of your community is eye-opening, comforting and grounding.

The DAC ladies who came forward when I called, and bravely shared their personal stories with me. Amanda, Anita, Anne, April, Che, Clare, Deb, Denise, Elly, Janet, Jeannie, Jenny, Joan, Joanne, Katherine, Kathy, Lyndall, Marion, Megan, Nadine, Nat and Sugar, along with Gillian from Colleen's Lingerie and Swimwear – a particular thank you for allowing me to share your wisdom in this book and to tell your stories in full in the next one. You all had a story to tell that will impact the hearts of others, and I was humbled by your honesty and openness.

Jane Turner, author coach (writewithjane.com) and wonderful friend. Every coach needs their own coach and you have been the best. Those long conversations where you just listened, popped in with pearls of wisdom and allowed me to waffle while I solved my dilemma – they were what got me through. Thank you also to Jane's team, cover designer Miriam Rudolf and layout artist Andrew Davies – without your expertise, the book would be little more than a Word document.

The cover photo of my tattoo was taken by the fabulous Mel Thornberry (melthornberryphotography.com) and the author photo on the back cover was taken by the equally fabulous Gray Tham (simplygray.com.au) as part of her Fifty & Wiser project. Both of you have the knack of making a person who really doesn't like posing for photos quite enjoy the experience. I love working with both of you for your energy, sense of humour and pure joy at what you do.

The tattoo itself, which sits on my left forearm, was designed and inked by the steady hand of the talented Heath Holloway, Two 9 Tattoo (two9tattoo.com) and Holloway Tattoo. I used to joke that I had three tattoos – the ones I got so they could line everything up for radiation. They hurt. Heath's tattoos didn't. When someone tells you that you can't just stop at one tattoo, believe them.

Megan Kelly, my copy editor (mkfictionediting.com). Your eye for detail is second to none. Thank you for retaining the voice in my story and ironing out all the typos and clunky sentences.

My husband Karl, daughter Ashlea and son Geordie. You weathered that year and put up with the aftermath … and all the lasagne. You were and are my strength.

My friends – both old and new – who give me space and accept who I am and what I say. You make me laugh and keep me sane.

My mum, Julie, who fact-checked what I wrote about my grandmother – and then went on to read the rest of the memoir for me. Having you read it ahead of time was a little nerve-wracking but also comforting, especially when you said you loved it.

My grandfather, Allan and dad, Peter – aka the blind and the breathless. I miss you both like you wouldn't believe. You always told me to believe in myself and encouraged me to pursue my dreams and tell my stories.

I'm sure the two of you were sitting with me the whole time I was writing this book. Odds are that you were also stirring the pot in your good-natured, and slightly annoying, way.

And, my nanna, Violet. Thank you for being my Oong-ga and being such a big part of my life for forty-eight years. I am honoured.

www.ingramcontent.com/pod-product-compliance
Lightning Source LLC
Chambersburg PA
CBHW020324010526
44107CB00054B/1962